Praise for *The Bromley Boys*

'Funny, wise and extremely charming.'
Guardian

'Reminds you of Danny Baker's *606* at its vintage best.'
Independent

'Genuinely funny . . . thoroughly recommended.'
When Saturday Comes

'This marvellous memoir is a must-read . . . exceedingly funny
. . . among the very best books with a sporting theme.'
Yorkshire Evening Post

'Agonisingly funny – perfectly captures the sad, futile, yet
glorious world of the adolescent male football fan.'
Harry Pearson, author of *The Far Corner* and *Dribble!*

'The best football memoir I have ever read. Dave Roberts
relates his story with irresistible charm and sharp, self-
deprecating wit . . . deserves to be a classic.'
Charlie Connelly, author of *Attention all Shipping* and *Stamping
Ground: Exploring Liechtenstein and Its World Cup Dream*

'Will strike a chord with football fans everywhere.'
Adrian Chiles

'I loved it . . . extremely funny. A must-read for anyone who
loves football.'
Peter Crouch

'Nothing has been as good as *Fever Pitch*. Until now. Laugh out
loud funny . . . a real treat.'
TheBookbag.co.uk

Also by Dave Roberts

The Bromley Boys
e-luv: an internet romance

32 Programmes

Dave Roberts

BANTAM PRESS

LONDON • TORONTO • SYDNEY • AUCKLAND • JOHANNESBURG

TRANSWORLD PUBLISHERS
61–63 Uxbridge Road, London W5 5SA
A Random House Group Company
www.rbooks.co.uk

First published in Great Britain
in 2011 by Bantam Press
an imprint of Transworld Publishers

A CIP catalogue record for this book
is available from the British Library.

ISBN 9780593067376

Addresses for Random House Group Ltd companies outside the UK
can be found at: www.randomhouse.co.uk
The Random House Group Ltd Reg. No. 954009

The Random House Group Ltd supports the Forest Stewardship
Council (FSC), the leading international forest-certification organization. All our
titles that are printed on Greenpeace-approved FSC-certified paper carry the FSC logo.
Our paper procurement policy can be found at
www.rbooks.co.uk/environment

Typeset in 12.5/15pt Erhhardt by
Falcon Oast Graphic Art Ltd.
Printed and bound in Great Britain by
CPI Mackays, Chatham, ME5 8TD

2 4 6 8 10 9 7 5 3 1

To my dad, Edward Roberts,
who bought me my first programme

The 32 Programmes

Prologue

I have a theory that the male of the species is programmed (sorry) to collect things. I had a wardrobe full of various collections by the time I reached my teenage years: oven-dried conkers, football cards, Matchbox cars, stamps, paper clips (don't ask), fossils, Captain Pugwash cartoons clipped from the *Radio Times*, and marbles. There was even a short-lived flirtation with bus tickets, which ended in humiliation when I proudly showed them to my unimpressed schoolmates. But these were mere test runs, honing my craft before discovering my true passion.

Football programmes.

A collection generally starts with a single item, and for me that was the programme for Fulham v. Manchester United in September 1964, when I was nine. It was a simple black-and-white affair made up mainly of blurred action shots and ads promoting cigarettes, beer and horse racing tipsters. Today's equivalent is more likely to be full colour, with advertisers trying to flog you expensive cars, airline deals and financial services – and nowhere near as exciting.

It didn't take long before I was hooked, buying two programmes every time I went to a game: one would be used for notes on the match, the other would join my collection. Over the years, I learned everything I could about them, and was surprised that they'd been around since the 1870s, although these were basically team sheets. The most astonishing discovery was that a 1923 Cup Final programme – the football programme world's equivalent of the penny black – would set you back around the same as a decent second-hand car. I'm just glad I never had to choose between the two.

As my collection grew, so did my understanding of why I was doing it. I loved being able to relive games at any time, as well as loosen memories of personal milestones I'd reached, especially during my formative years. It was as though I owned a part of every game I'd been to.

Then, in late 2008, my wife and I decided to move to the US. The plan was to stay with her parents for a while, while we found jobs and a house to rent. We decided to put most of our stuff into storage until we found somewhere permanent to live and take only what was 'absolutely essential'. I assumed she would see that my programme collection fell into this category, but alarm bells started ringing when I saw her approaching as I was carefully placing them in a suitcase.

'So how many of these were you thinking of taking?' she asked.

'All of them,' I replied, surprised that anyone could think otherwise. 'They're my football programmes.'

'And where are we going to put everything else?' she demanded, as though she was asking a perfectly reasonable question.

'Well, do we have to take all those clothes?' I suggested.

Her look signalled to me that the answer was yes.

'What about these, then?' I said, holding up a thick file. 'They're just papers, aren't they?'

'Well, I guess we could leave our passports, birth certificates and bank papers behind if it means you'll be able to take more football programmes.'

My initial joy at this response faded rapidly when I realized she was probably being sarcastic.

It was eventually agreed that I would take a Tupperware container the size of a Dan Brown hardback and put as many programmes in it as I could manage, without risking bending or creasing. The problem was that, according to my extensive testing process, it only had room for between twenty-five and thirty-five programmes, depending on thickness. My collection numbered 1,134 (serious enthusiasts are sticklers for precision) spread over a dozen shoeboxes.

I would therefore only be able to take the ones that meant something really special, from the programme of my very first match to the one signed by the greatest player in the world. Some of the choices (like these) were easy, but you can't possibly know the true meaning of angst unless you've been forced to choose between Norway v. England (1981) and Crystal Palace v. Manchester United (1972). After a restless night, I decided on the latter, although I'm still not sure I made the right decision.

Going through each of the 1,134 programmes brought back a flood of nostalgia for simpler times. Some I hadn't read in years, and I was surprised that the sights and smells from those games were still so fresh in my mind. Although I had started out with the intention of simply taking the programmes that were the most valuable, my criteria slowly started to shift. It was the ones with the most dramatic memories, both on and off the field, that were making the cut.

Finally, with just a few hours to go before our flight, I had narrowed down the most important programmes in my life to thirty-one, which filled that Tupperware container to the brim. Since moving, I have added one more to the collection – one I never thought I would see and which means more to me than any other. But since this book is in chronological order, I've saved that until last.

So, why did I choose these thirty-two programmes over all the others? Here are the stories behind each one – and a whole lot more besides.

32 Programmes

FULHAM FOOTBALL CLUB

official programme 6d

SEASON 1964-5 LEAGUE DIVISION ONE

MANCHESTER UNITED

SATURDAY 5 SEPTEMBER 1964 KICK-OFF 3 PM

1

Fulham v. Manchester United, 5 September 1964

If any player is worth his weight in gold it must be fair-haired Denis Law, the Master forward in Manchester United's strong attack.

From the official programme

Most boys inherit a love of football from their fathers and therefore a passion for the sport, as well as the choice of team, is usually predetermined. Not me. My dad hated football. He was a quiet, refined man, more at home with his books or pottering around the garden. But he knew how much it meant to me. And that was why, when I was nine and a half, he surprised me by taking me to see Fulham against Manchester United, two of my many favourite teams.

As we walked along Fulham Palace Road and down Bishop's Park Road, the anticipation was almost overwhelming. For the past few days I had traced the route with my index finger over and over again on the *A–Z*, memorizing every street and turning. My football watching had been limited to local park games and a new programme called *Match of the Day* on TV. Now that I was going to see a proper match for the first time I was so excited that I hadn't eaten all day. I couldn't wait to get to Fulham's Craven Cottage ground, although I was happy to stop along the way to pick up a couple of official programmes from a man with OFFICIAL PROGRAMME SELLER on his coat.

Soon we came across another distraction, in the form of a stand selling rosettes. I had to have one. The only problem was that, as my dad yet again reached into his pocket for some change, I was torn by indecision.

'Which team are you supporting?' he asked me.

I thought about this. A small queue waited for me to make up my mind.

'Manchester United,' I said eventually, without conviction.

Before the man had a chance to hand over the red rosette, I had a change of heart. 'No, Fulham,' I said, swayed by the fact that everyone walking past seemed to have a black and white scarf.

'Are you sure?'

'No, not really,' I replied. 'Manchester United.' I was thinking about all their players whose pictures were on my bedroom wall.

I swayed from one option to the other for about a minute. Eventually, Dad wearily handed over the money for one of each, the black and white of Fulham and the red and white of Manchester United, both of which I proudly affixed to my shirt.

I had heroes on both sides. Rodney Marsh, the lanky young Fulham centre-forward who refused to tuck his shirt in, was my joint favourite footballer. It was because of him that I went to school one day with my shirt hanging outside my shorts and my hair not brushed, which resulted in me getting told off and having to tidy myself up. Another joint favourite footballer was also playing. Denis Law was, by coincidence, another forward who didn't like tucking his shirt in. I modelled my game on him, especially his ability to soar into the air. I practised jumping as high as I could for hours on end and only stopped when my calves hurt too much to carry on.

Just as we were about to turn the corner into Stevenage Road, I saw a trader's stall that brought me to a sudden halt. Pinned to a large piece of cardboard were red star-shaped badges the size of a penny coin, each of which contained a black and white photo of one of the Manchester club's stars. Even more thrillingly, they were autographed, although I did wonder why the players had identical handwriting. I quickly used up all my pocket money on Denis Law, Bobby Charlton, John Connelly and David Sadler badges. I was running out of available space on my shirtfront, but managed to find a place for all four of them.

As Craven Cottage approached, the crowd was being expertly controlled by a handful of policemen on what seemed from my youthful perspective to be giant grey horses with nostrils the size of saucers. They were so much bigger than any horses I had ever seen, and I convinced myself that they must have been specially bred for police duty.

Going through the turnstile for the first time made me feel all grown up. Dad handed over the money and we were in. We climbed the steps and took our places on the crowded terrace where, strangely, most spectators had their backs to the pitch, preferring to watch the rowers go through their paces on the Thames. Not me, though. I read the programme from cover to cover, staring at the names in the team line-ups on the centre pages and imagining them in action. I was also really pleased to see that Johnny Haynes liked Wembley vinyl footballs so much that he was in an advert for them. I'd recently got one and thought it was great, too.

Suddenly, a roar startled me out of my thoughts. The crowd

had got their first sight of the players coming out on to the pitch and the atmosphere in the ground came alive, as though someone had suddenly switched the electricity on.

I was immediately caught up in the emotion. 'Johnny Haynes!' I screamed in a high-pitched voice, pointing to the Fulham number 10. 'That's Johnny Haynes!'

My dad had the good grace to pretend he hadn't recognized one of England's most famous faces.

I saw another familiar figure. 'Rodney Marsh! Look, Rodney Marsh!'

When the United team ran out I was struck by how bright their red shirts were, having only seen them in slightly blurry black and white on television. 'Denis Law!' I shrieked, by now feeling light-headed with excitement. 'Bobby Charlton! There's Bobby Charlton!' I was jumping up and down, screaming out the names of all the players I recognized as they emerged from under the Bovril sign.

The teams were greeted by a beautiful autumn day. The flags were perfectly still, the sun was strong, and most of the crowd were in their shirtsleeves. It hadn't rained for ages. All around me rattles were producing a deafeningly loud cacophony which made it even harder to catch the attention of the peanut vendor, who was weaving his way through the crowd, tempting us with his cries of 'Lovely hot peanuts! Fresh roasted peanuts!' If he couldn't reach you, you passed the threepence down to him through the hands of dozens of fellow supporters and he passed the peanuts back using the same method. Dad bought me a bag, slightly concerned that I hadn't had breakfast or lunch.

As I was stuffing my mouth full of nuts, I heard a few snatches of a conversation between some people behind us. I learned that Tony Dunne, United's left-back, had been sick overnight and had had such a high temperature that he had been in doubt until kick-off. I hoped he was feeling better. I wanted to see a fair match.

Then the referee blew his whistle for the start of the game. I didn't know it yet, but it also signalled the beginning of a lifetime's obsession with watching football. And there was something else I couldn't have known at the time: most of the games I saw would be played at a far lower level than this one.

With less than a minute gone, the ball went out of play and I shouted, 'Offside!' My grasp of the rules was not yet complete and I was convinced that if the ball went off the side of the pitch, it was offside. By the time I'd worked out that I was the only one shouting offside when this happened, I plucked up the courage to ask my dad. He admitted that he didn't know, but thought too it might be when the ball went off the side of the pitch.

The first shot of the game, from John Connelly, was so wide that it hit the *Daily Express* sign with a thud, giving the photographers sitting around it in their suits and ties a real fright. Then Tony Dunne took a throw. Or tried to. It was so bad the referee whistled for a foul throw. Dunne was probably still ill.

Just as I was wondering what Fremlin's was (there was a giant sign behind the Fulham goal saying DRINK FREMLIN'S), the first major incident of the match took place right in front of us. George Cohen committed a terrible foul on George Best that must have really hurt, but the United winger, who was only eighteen, just got up and carried on. I envied him. The last time I'd played in the playground I was fouled and had grazed my knee. I'd hobbled off to the first-aid room desperately trying to hold back the tears.

Then, out of the blue, came the moment I had dreamed about: my first goal. David Sadler scored it with a fabulous strike from just inside the penalty area. It was the most thrilling thing I had ever seen. I was jumping around, feeling as though I could burst from all the excitement.

When I got my breath back I noticed that the players weren't running back to halfway or shaking hands with one another. Instead, Tony Macedo, Fulham's goalie, was taking a free kick. The goal had been disallowed, and judging from the cries of 'Offside!' from everyone around us, I suspected that was the reason. I noticed my dad was deep in conversation with an older man standing next to him and he was nodding along as the man talked, using his hands to explain what he meant. Dad then turned to me and said that he had asked about the offside law. It was something about players having to be between the goalscorer and the goal when the ball was passed. I was really grateful that he'd found out for me, but I didn't think either of us was any closer to understanding.

There were no cries for offside when John Connelly scored a proper goal not long after. 'GOAL!' I shrieked, keeping a close eye on the referee in case it was offside and I had to stop jumping around. But this time he pointed to the halfway line and I knew, beyond doubt, that United had taken the lead.

They continued to attack when the second half got underway. Connelly took another shot and, like in the first half, hit the *Daily Express* sign. Then Denis Law put the ball in the net, but the mysterious offside rule again cut short the celebrations. The equalizer came as Fulham were starting to look the better side. Rodney Marsh beat the diving Gaskell with a great shot and Nobby Stiles and Shay Brennan, running back, combined to help the ball into their own net. It was 1–1.

It was as if the stage was being set for Johnny Haynes, who gave Fulham the lead following a great through-ball from yet another of my favourite players, Bobby Robson. It was a beautifully taken goal and one the supporters who had left early would have missed. There were only minutes left on the giant clock on the roof of the stand.

The Fulham fans around us were now whistling, in case the referee had forgotten to look at his watch. I tried to join in, but I couldn't really whistle so ended up puffing up my cheeks and making a blowing kind of noise, hoping no one would notice.

While this was going on, a Bobby Charlton thunderbolt was tipped round the post by Macedo. The ball bounced towards a man in rolled-up shirtsleeves and braces with a cigarette hanging from his mouth, who was sitting in a chair near the corner flag. Although he looked a bit put out at having to leave the comfort of his chair, he stood up, caught the ball (at the second attempt) and handed it to John Connelly.

Connelly's corner was a good one. Denis Law leapt at the far post, headed the ball down and Bill Foulkes (a former coalminer, according to the programme) tapped it home. I felt a mix of emotions. My United supporting side was happy, my Fulham side frustrated.

These positions were reversed a few seconds later when the referee disallowed the goal and gave a free kick, ruling that Law had fouled Macedo. The Fulham fans began booing Law for his unsportsmanlike behaviour, which I felt more comfortable joining in with, even though I really liked him, as it was a lot easier than whistling.

There was no time for any more and the referee blew for full time. My first proper match was over, and it was time to go home. As we headed back down the stairs, Dad reached for my hand, but in the last two hours I had become too grown up to take it. I was old enough to go to football now, so I confidently made my own way out.

I was enjoying the sensation of being swept along by the crowd, my dad next to me, talking about football. But then, in a split second, we were separated as I was caught up in a wave of people heading in the opposite direction. I was being carried away from the ground, away from my dad, helpless to do anything about it. As he disappeared from view, I just wanted to go back, but couldn't. The momentum of the crowd was too strong. My heart was thudding against my chest wall with fear. I shouted for him, but had little chance of being heard above the noise.

It wasn't until we were a couple of hundred yards away from the stadium that the throng thinned enough for me to duck out and press myself against a wall. I glanced up the road, back to where I'd just come from, hoping to see Dad, but he wasn't there. I felt in a state of blind panic and would have given anything – my rosettes, my badges, even my precious programmes – to find him. I started to run blindly, back in the direction of the tube station.

And then, at the corner of Stevenage Road and Bishop's Park Road, I saw him, talking to one of the policemen on horseback. I ran over to him, grabbed his hand and didn't let go until we were safely on the tube.

Later that night, my parents said I could stay up and we could watch the game again on *Match of the Day* and maybe catch a glimpse of ourselves in the crowd. I'd glanced over at Dad a couple of times during the game and seen that his mind was elsewhere; to voluntarily sit through it all again showed how lucky I was to have him for my dad. I loved reliving the highlights and kept telling him what was about to happen, even though he probably had a pretty good idea.

Over the next two years I felt I was growing up quickly. Although I still went to matches with my dad – usually to Fulham, as I suspected he liked to watch the boats on the Thames while I watched the football – some of my friends were going to places like Stamford Bridge and Highbury on their own. At least that's what they told me. And then, in the holiday between primary school and secondary school, I was given the chance to visit England's most glamorous football city. On my own.

UNITED REVIEW

MANCHESTER UNITED FOOTBALL CLUB

MANCHESTER
UNITED
v.
CHELSEA
Kick-off 3-0 pm

SATURDAY
18th SEPTEMBER

6d.

NUMBER 6

1965-66

SEASON

OFFICIAL　　　　　**PROGRAMME**

BURNLEY v. UNITED – SEPTEMBER 11th, 1965

Here Burnley goalkeeper Thomson having failed to gather a shot from Best is confronted by United's David Herd. Burnley full-back Elder, however, (centre) scrambled the ball clear. Burnley ran out the winners by three clear goals.　　　　Photograph by courtesy of the Seddon Press Agency, Burnley

2

Manchester United v. Chelsea, 18 September 1965

One player who will be hoping to get on the scoresheet today is Denis Law, who needs just one goal to reach 50 for the club.

From the official programme

I felt my heart lurch when I stepped off the train and set foot in Manchester for the first time. To me, at the age of eleven, it was the most exciting place on earth. Not only was it the home of Manchester United *and* Manchester City, but also Herman's Hermits and The Hollies. My dad had put me on the train at Euston and I was met at Manchester Piccadilly station by my parents' friend, who I would be staying with for a week during the holidays. She insisted on me calling her Jennifer, which I found a bit embarrassing. I think I would have preferred Mrs Gardener.

As we drove through the city centre, I looked out of the rain-flecked window, hoping to catch a glimpse of Denis Law, George Best or even Shay Brennan, walking the streets doing their shopping. But apart from someone who looked a bit like left-back Tony Dunne, but was much too old, I was out of luck.

The Gardeners lived in a huge, rambling house in a suburb called Chorlton-cum-Hardy, which had posters in the front windows protesting against all sorts of things: Vietnam, South African oranges and experiments on animals among others. They even had a doorknocker in the shape of the Ban the Bomb symbol, and a collection tin for Oxfam just inside the front door. Mr Gardener, who wanted me to call him Colin, had grey hair that went over his collar at the back, and tufts of black hair growing out of his nose. There were five children, although one had left home; I'd be staying in his room. The other four were all older than me and hardly ever around.

I lugged my BOAC bag (a souvenir of the previous year's holiday in Switzerland) upstairs and unpacked, neatly folding my clothes and putting them in the drawers, like my mum had told me to do. I then put my transistor radio on the bedside table.

About this time I became aware of a constant, strangely familiar, thudding sound coming from outside. I looked out of the window and noticed a scruffy boy of around my age kicking a plastic ball against a garage door, which had the shape of a goal painted on it. After each goal he wheeled away and, his sleeves gripped tightly in his fists, raised his right arm to the air, index finger extended, in celebration.

My mouth was gaping and my pulse racing with excitement. He was doing exactly what I did when I scored a goal in the playground back at home. This could only mean one thing.

I dashed downstairs, through the back door and round the corner, where I came face to face with the boy.

'Hello. Umm . . . do you like Denis Law?' I asked, slightly out of breath.

'The Lawman?' he replied, his face lighting up. 'Yeah, he's my hero.'

'Mine too. I call him The King.'

Although we had slightly different nicknames for him, we agreed on how great he was. This was enough to seal an instant friendship.

'So, fancy a kickabout? My name's Dave.'

'Pahl.'

'Pardon?'

'Pahl – that's me name.'

And with that, we played one-on-one for the next few hours, each goal from either of us celebrated in exactly the same way. With the Denis Law one-armed salute. At one point I shoulder-charged him and he immediately yelled out in pain. He must have hurt his arm somehow as I could see a bit of bruising under his shirt. I asked him what the matter was, but he didn't say anything.

When it got dark, we sat outside and swapped Denis Law stories. I told him about seeing Denis play at Fulham and how he'd set up that disallowed late goal. Pahl said he'd seen most United home games in the last three seasons so had seen a bit more of him than me. I ran upstairs and got my Manchester United badges out of my bag, to show my new friend. He liked them so much I decided to give him the Bobby Charlton one.

That night, over a dinner of nut roast, I asked Mrs Gardener if they knew Pahl. She exchanged glances with her husband.

'You mean Paul from a few doors down?'

'Yes,' I replied, trying to cover up for the fact that I'd been confused by Paul's Manchester accent. 'He's great. I played with him today.'

'That's nice.'

They told me that his parents had split up and he lived with his dad, who didn't work. Paul had told them that he had two paper rounds and they often saw him sitting on the wall out-side, late at night, doing nothing. I wondered why he didn't stay at home and watch TV or listen to music.

The next morning, there was a knock on the door. It was Paul. He had a box under his arm and when I asked what it was he said it was his collection of grms. 'Grms – you know, programmes.' We went into the kitchen, where he proudly showed me his grms. Every single one. I had never seen anything like it. The United grm was called *The United Review* and featured a bad drawing of a man in a suit shaking hands with a United player. He even had loads of United reserves grms, which had an even worse drawing on the front, this time of two players chasing a ball. Paul had dozens of them, and I gazed at them enviously.

He shyly handed one over to me – Manchester United v. Chelsea from the previous season. As we both knew, this was an extremely special grm as Denis Law had scored a hat-trick in the match.

'Go on, take it,' Paul said. 'I've got two. I was only keeping that for swapsies.'

As I gratefully took it, he whispered in a voice so quiet I could barely hear, 'If I told you something would you promise not to tell anyone? Cross your heart and hope to die?'

I quickly went through the motions of crossing my heart, desperate to hear his secret.

He leaned closer and whispered seven words which had a similar impact on me to being struck by lightning: 'I know where The Lawman's house is.'

This was news that my brain was barely able to process. He told me that one of the boys he went to school with lived in the same street and had given Denis Law's address to Paul in exchange for a Bounty bar. I asked him if it would be OK with his dad if we went there on our own the next morning, but he just shrugged his shoulders.

I packed my Manchester United v. Chelsea grm, together with two pens (in case one didn't work), and was ready to go when Paul knocked on the door at eleven the following day, having finished both of his paper rounds. He was hungry so insisted on getting a late breakfast of 'chips and vee' before we set off. By now I'd worked out his way of talking and had a good idea that 'vee' was gravy. I wondered if gravy had meat in it, as I'd decided to be a vegetarian for the week. It was a bit of a grey area, but it was so delicious I decided it was probably OK.

We got on the bus, climbed upstairs and paid the conductor. I could tell how far away we were from our destination by Paul's left leg, which shook more and more the nearer we got. It was resembling a pneumatic drill by the time he announced that we'd be getting off at the next stop.

After a short walk along a row of similar-looking houses, we came to a halt. 'This one,' said Paul, with a shaky voice.

It was here that our courage deserted us completely. While it had been great talking about and imagining what it would be like knocking on the door of Denis Law's house, actually doing it was much harder – even though neither of us totally believed Paul's friend's story about living in the same street as the best footballer in the world. I'd always imagined he lived in a palace with servants, not a terraced house in Manchester.

Finally, Paul knocked on the door. This was either going to be really embarrassing or one of the best moments of our lives.

A friendly woman in a sundress with shortish curly dark hair opened it, a quizzical look breaking out on her face as she found herself looking down at a couple of red-faced boys, each clutching a Manchester United v. Chelsea grm from the 1965/66 season. Neither of us could speak. Behind her, we could just about make out a familiar slender figure lurking in the background. Or were we imagining it?

We were left in no doubt when Denis Law, fists not gripping the sleeves of his V-necked pullover, strode to the door, smiling.

'Hello, lads,' he said, in a Scottish accent, as the woman went back inside.

I soon discovered how quickly confidence evaporates when you meet your heroes. We stood there gaping, unable to find words. Luckily, he didn't have the same problem.

'United fans, are you?'

We both nodded eagerly, desperately trying to think of something to say.

Eventually, Paul found his voice. 'Can you sign my grm please, Mr Law? Can you say "To Paul"?'

The King took it, rested it against the wall and did as he'd been asked.

As Paul's approach had worked, I decided to use the same words. 'Can you sign *my* grm please, Mr Law?' I said, handing it to him. 'My name's Dave.'

'To Dave' he wrote on the back, where the teams were, 'Best Wishes Denis Law'.

He seemed like a normal person and I vowed to follow his example if I ever became a famous footballer. Considering that kids knocking on his door must have happened all the time, he seemed genuinely pleased to see us and was happy to give us his autograph. We really didn't want to leave, but it didn't seem fair on the Law family for us to just stand there and stare at Denis all afternoon, so we reluctantly turned and walked away, after thanking him far too many times. For the entire bus journey home each of us was in his own little world, stunned at what had just taken place.

When I got back, I compared the autograph with the writing on my badge. It was completely different. I put the grm on my bedside table and arranged it in such a way that I could stare at it with my head rested on the pillow. It was amazing how a simple two-second scrawl could be the cause of such deep happiness.

The next day, Paul knocked on the door early, as usual, wearing the same clothes he usually wore. Mrs Gardener offered him breakfast, which he was really happy to have, as he seemed quite hungry. For the next few days he pretty much lived with us. I loved having such a good friend with me, especially one who wanted to do nothing but play football and talk about football.

When the week was up, Paul asked Mrs Gardener if he could come to the station when they dropped me off. They were happy to do it even though our constant discussions about Manchester United players must have been driving them mad.

Paul looked really sad as he solemnly stuck out his hand and we shook to say goodbye. He made me promise to keep in touch, so I put his name and address in my address book. Just after Denis Law's.

When I got home I continued to go to matches with my dad, and over the next few years he took me to matches all over London. I suspected, or rather hoped, that he was developing a liking for the game. We saw some of the biggest names in the game, like Jimmy Greaves, Peter Osgood, George Eastham and Ron Flowers. I soon filled a scrapbook with newspaper reports of matches we'd seen together. And every game we went to, I always made sure I got a spare grm to send to Paul.

When, eventually, I was old enough to go to games on my own, I sensed Dad was relieved, although perhaps a little sad. Both he and my mum didn't want me going to First Division games, following the scare at Craven Cottage, but they were perfectly happy for me to go along and support our local non-league team, Bromley, on my own; anywhere else, and I had to go with an adult.

The first time I'd gone to a game with an adult other than Dad was when I went to a fixture that was so low key, most people didn't even know it was on: England against Germany in 1966 at Wembley.

SCHOOLS' INTERNATIONAL

(Under the auspices of the English Schools' Football Association)

Saturday, April 30th 1966. Kick-off 3 p.m.

W E M B L E Y

EMPIRE STADIUM

ENGLAND
v
GERMANY

Official Programme · One Shilling

3

England Schools v. Germany Schools, 30 April 1966

Your encouragement and conduct will contribute to the atmosphere of the game. May you thoroughly enjoy yourselves and vow to return either as spectators or perhaps players. I must pay special tribute to the many teachers who have organised parties, especially those who have done so for a number of years.

From the official programme

I'd overslept, which meant I was the last one to climb on to the coach for our school outing to Wembley. The occasion was a schoolboys international between England and Germany, and there was a buzz of excited chatter from the thirty or so eleven-year-olds on board, relishing the chance to get away without their parents.

I felt rising panic as I looked around for somewhere to sit. The only spare seat appeared to be next to Susan, the only girl going to the match and someone I thought about pretty much constantly, especially after hearing the rumour that she wore a bra. I felt my face flush and heartbeat quicken, terrified at the prospect of sitting next to a girl I really liked, and was massively relieved to spot a space at the back, next to my friend Russell.

As I passed Susan, I coughed theatrically, in a manner that was meant to attract her attention without looking as though I was trying to attract her attention. I wanted her to glance up and see me, because if she did she would see that I was wearing my official Batman utility belt to the match. It held a complete set of crime fighting equipment: a bat signal flash, a bat rope, a bat-a-rang, a bat rocket grenade, bat cuffs, a Batman message sender (which looked uncannily like the bat rocket grenade) and a bat gun launcher. There was also a secret storage compartment where I kept my bat sweets and bat spending money.

It made me feel, and quite probably look, like Batman. Never once had I questioned how you were supposed to scale tall buildings with what appeared to be an eighteen-inch piece of thickish string, or contact Commissioner Gordon with a tiny torch that was barely powerful enough to use for reading under my bed covers.

The utility belt had cost me nearly a month's pocket money, but it had been worth it. It was slightly tight round my waist, admittedly, but otherwise hugely impressive. Unfortunately Susan seemed to be engrossed in the exercise book that was open on her lap, but I was confident there would be other opportunities to show her my crime fighting equipment during the day.

As well as Susan, I was also desperate to impress Russell – although not quite in the same way. As soon as he saw the belt, I knew I had succeeded. Admiration was written all over his face.

'Go on, try it on,' I offered generously, undoing the clip and handing him the belt.

Russell was one of the best footballers in the school and

therefore someone I was eager to befriend. Since I couldn't do this with my footballing ability, I had decided to take a different tack. He put it on, jumped up and adopted a Batman fighting pose, which lost its impact when the belt slipped to the floor. Apparently there was a slight difference in our waist sizes and since neither of us could work out how to adjust what purported to be an adjustable belt, I put it back on.

The rest of the trip passed with mounting excitement and the chatter grew higher and higher pitched. Some of the boys couldn't sit still and were pacing restlessly up and down the aisle. Every sighting of a road sign that mentioned Wembley was greeted with loud cheers.

We finally arrived at 1.15, pulled into the car park right in front of the enormous twin towers and poured out on to the tarmac. There were thousands of people just milling around. The sun was shining, and the sky was cloudless. It was a perfect day for watching football.

I removed three shillings from my utility belt and handed them over to one of the programme sellers in exchange for two programmes: one to use during the match, and one for my fledgling collection. I managed to resist the temptations of the rosette, flag and rattle vendors, but the ice-cream man had me reaching, once again, for my utility belt.

After briefly stopping off at the Royal Engineers recruitment stand in the car park, we went through the turnstiles. My first sight of the pitch made my legs tremble, because it looked so green and perfect. I couldn't take my eyes off it, even as Mr Barrett, our teacher, was escorting us to our seats in a stand by one of the corner flags. I was lost in a fantasy in which I was running down the wing in front of a packed Wembley, before sending in a perfect cross for Jimmy Greaves to head home the winning goal in the World Cup Final, which would be played in a couple of months' time.

The World Cup had also provided me with another fantasy: finding the man who had recently stolen it from Westminster Central Hall and slapping my bat cuffs on him. Police had described the thief as being in his early thirties, of average height with thin lips, greased black hair and a possible scar on his face. I was constantly on the lookout for him, even though the trophy had already been found by Pickles the dog.

When I returned to reality, I sat down in my allocated seat. Although the view wasn't ideal, I was delighted to be just one seat away from Susan, which was just near enough to bask in her presence and just far away enough to avoid embarrassment.

I got my programme out and carefully read through it. The teams didn't mean anything to me as I'd never heard of any of the players, but after going through the pen portraits I picked a few favourites. Alan Mitchell (Liverpool) sounded interesting. He was 'very mobile, a good header of the ball, plenty of moral fibre'. I also liked the sound of Stephen Wilkinson (Stoke): a 'very swift mover, uses the ball to bring wingers into the game'. As a winger myself, I appreciated that. The main threat from the Germans appeared to come from Kurt Tinurski (TSV Marl-Huels), who was described as being 'physically strong, good shot. A dashing player who does not shirk physical contact, difficult to dispossess and never giving up.' Pretty much the opposite of me, I thought.

Just as I was about to turn to the next page I heard a sound that filled me with horror. It started with a solitary drum beating, and this was soon joined by a mass of trumpets. I looked out on to the pitch and saw a brass band in red uniforms and black busbies marching in perfect time out of the tunnel as they played 'When the Saints Go Marching In'.

'Oh no!' I said loudly to Martin, who was sitting next to me. 'I really hate brass bands.'

'Yeah, me too,' came agreement from an unexpected quarter.

It was Susan! She was speaking to me! And she was agreeing with me! We had something in common!

I desperately tried to think of a way to build on this platform and demonstrate just how much I hated brass bands, but came up empty. I reached into my utility belt for a piece of Juicy Fruit chewing gum, as this was meant to help concentration, but it didn't inspire me.

After half an hour of tedious music it still wasn't time for football. Instead we were treated to a physical training display by junior soldiers, which looked less like a display and more like watching hundreds of boys doing PE. Every face in our row of seats looked bored, as though they realized that they had been brought to Wembley under false pretences. Even a display by the Royal Signals Motorcycle Display Team failed to lift the collective mood.

Then, at precisely 2.30, came the moment I'd been waiting for. Not the football, but the community singing. Finally, I had another chance to impress Susan. As everyone stood up to sing, I made a big show of putting down on my seat the *Daily Express* Community Singing sheet, which had the words to all the songs. This was meant to signal (to Susan) that I didn't need it as I knew all the songs in the hit parade off by heart.

As the man in the white suit waved his baton in the direction of yet another brass band, I took a deep breath and launched into Dusty Springfield's 'You Don't Have to Say You Love Me'. I sang as loudly as I could and was sure Susan had been able to hear me. I felt that I'd done reasonably well, apart from singing 'believe me' one too many times. Next up was 'Tears' by Ken Dodd, which I also knew off by heart, then something called 'Keep Right On to the End of the Road', which I had to improvise.

The community singing reached the end of the road after that, and both teams trotted out into the spring sunshine. By the time the Rt Hon. Dr Horace King MP, Speaker of the House of Commons, left the field after shaking hands with every single player and official, there was a cacophony of noise all around the stadium as if everyone was coming back to life after the endless build-up and formalities.

What immediately became apparent, as soon as the game kicked off, was that the schoolboys played at a much faster pace than their senior counterparts. England were on top for much of the first half, but couldn't convert any of their many chances.

The game was half an hour old when I was presented with another chance to impress Susan. It happened just after Germany had taken an unexpected lead through right-back Rainer Hoppe (Walsum 09). After checking out of the corner of my eye that she was still there, I shouted in the direction of Hoppe, who was standing about twenty yards away: 'Oi, number zwei – sie sind ein schweinhund!'

The impression I wanted to give her was that I spoke fluent German, but had been too modest to mention it. The truth was that I'd picked up a few phrases from my favourite comic character, Captain Hurricane in the *Valiant*. He was frequently captured by the Nazis, whose dialogue was generally restricted to phrases such as 'donner und blitzen'; when the Captain and his sidekick Maggot Malone escaped their clutches with a show of superhuman strength, 'sie sind ein schweinhund' was their all-purpose insult. I could also count to five in German, although I could only do it backwards. This was because Captain Hurricane had once counted down in German before launching into one of his fearsome and destructive 'ragin' furies'.

My insult hurled at the German number two had the desired effect, even though he seemed unfazed by it.

'What did you say to him?' asked several of my impressed classmates at once.

'Oh, that?' I said modestly. 'I just called him a pigdog.'

It was at least ten minutes before my heart rate returned to normal. I had rarely felt so good as when my friends had lavished praise on me over my non-existent language skills.

On the field, things were getting frustrating for England. Despite having most of the ball, an equalizer eluded them, and as the whistle went for half time Germany were holding on to their 1–0 lead. Things took a turn for the worse before the second half even started as out of the tunnel and into the daylight emerged yet another brass band, this time for a display of marching and counter-marching. I managed to catch Susan's eye and tutted, while looking at the heavens. She tutted back, also looking upwards. I loved our shared dislike of brass bands.

The players eventually returned, and finally, with twenty minutes left, L. Hughes (Smethwick) slung over a low cross and Wilkinson, who had made such an impression in the programme notes, volleyed past Biermann for a spectacular equalizer. A minute later Hughes was in action at the other end, tripping Ungerwitter as he bore into the area. The referee, Mr Willis of Durham, did the distinctly unpatriotic thing and awarded a penalty. The German captain Sobieray took the kick, which was brilliantly saved by the diving S. Bowtell (East London), who immediately launched an attack that nearly led to a dramatic second goal for Wilkinson.

It was so exciting we were all now standing on our seats, shouting ourselves hoarse, willing our country towards victory. And it seemed to do the trick. England's winner came late in the game, when a cross from P. Lowery (Newcastle upon Tyne) was stylishly converted by D. Thomas (Bishop Auckland), the tricky winger (and SW Durham 220 yards junior sprint champion) who had already become my favourite player on the pitch. As the ball slowly crossed the line, the stadium erupted in a high-pitched squeal. England had grabbed a victory right at the death.

As we got on the coach, the mood was one of exhaustion. People were flopped in their seats and there was none of the standing or excited chatter that had marked the journey there. A few of the boys even fell asleep. I slumped down next to Russell and finally worked out how to loosen my utility belt, an action that had become a necessity after scoffing three ice-creams. The game had been incredibly entertaining and I couldn't imagine the senior England and Germany teams playing a more dramatic, exciting match that year or any other year.

There was one more thing that happened that day, to make it almost perfect. As I was about to be dropped off at the end of my road, Susan caught me looking at her. She smiled and said, 'See ya, Dave.'

I turned bright red, but managed to retain my composure enough to impress her one last time, by saying goodbye in what I felt was perfect German. 'Danke schön, mein Herr,' I said, stepping off the coach.

My first visit to Wembley had been an incredible experience. In my mind, only one stadium would ever make a bigger impression. And that was the one I was about to visit next.

SWANSEA CITY A.F.C.

SEASON 1970-71

GILLINGHAM

SATURDAY OCTOBER 24th, 1970
K.O. 3.0. p.m.   No. 9   1/-

4

Swansea City v. Gillingham,
24 October 1970

The Directors wish to thank CLIVE ALAN SIMCOCK
Builders, Treboeth, for the gift of the ball used in today's game.

From the official programme

To an outsider, Bromley FC's home at Hayes Lane was a moderate, slightly gone-to-seed non-league ground in a fairly dull South London suburb, but to me it was the centre of the football universe. I'd been a regular there since first being allowed to go on my own, and now, at the age of fifteen, I'd achieved my life's ambition and was working in the supporters' club shop. We sold Bromley pens and badges, and to pad out this meagre range of souvenirs, customers could also buy programmes from past league and non-league matches. These were surprisingly popular and I usually bought at least four every week, although I was getting a bit fed up with reading the same *Football League Review*, a magazine that was incorporated into just about all league programmes.

Before the vital Hitchin Town game (in my mind, all Bromley games were vital, and remain so to this day), Derek, treasurer of the supporters' club, had given me the job of unpacking a brand-new delivery of programmes and putting them out on the counter. I opened the box and stared at the awe-inspiring sight of hundreds of neatly packed programmes from all over the country. There were ones from the recent Oswestry Town v. Preston friendly, a routine Fourth Division clash between Southport and Bradford City, a schoolboys' game between England and Wales. I briefly studied each one, weighing up whether to buy it for my collection, before reluctantly adding them to my neat display.

But then I came across one that I had to check and re-check, to make sure I wasn't imagining things. It was for the Swansea Town v. Gillingham game of 24 October 1970. But on the cover was a catastrophic misprint. Instead of Swansea Town, it said Swansea City.

As a serious stamp collector, I felt I understood the value of misprints. The 1918 American twenty-four-cent stamp, printed with an upside down biplane, was worth thousands of pounds. When I was eleven I'd spent a significant proportion of my pocket money on packs of assorted stamps advertised in the back pages of the *Valiant* comic ('Free – over 200 different colourful stamps'), hoping to come across one, but hadn't had any luck. I'd even decided to increase my odds by sending off for approval packs from every advertiser, so off went a flurry of letters all over the country, to Bayona Stamps in Cheshire (Dept. V 51), Sterling Stamp Service in Sussex (Dept. V) and J. A. L. Franks Ltd (Dept. V) in London. All promised free worldwide stamps in return for a fourpenny stamp, and I felt that somewhere among them I would find my 1918 rarity.

But after sifting through literally thousands of worthless stamps, which I'd had to pay for since I never returned the approval packs on time, I'd drawn a blank. Actually, they weren't *totally* worthless: I'd taken most of them to my favourite dealer in Penge and he had offered me threepence for the entire collection, meaning a loss of around a hundred thousand per cent, which I felt was acceptable.

Now that disappointment was suddenly a distant memory as I found myself staring at something that could be just as valuable as that elusive biplane stamp. A programme with an incredible misprint.

I had to make sure it was the same Swansea, and this was confirmed by the team line-up on the back. It had all of Swansea Town's famous names, like goalie Tony Millington, centre-half Mel Nurse and tricky winger Len Allchurch. A quick flick through the programme provided plenty more evidence. There was even a table from 1925/26 (reprinted in honour of their 'magnificent first season in Division Two'), and in fifth place was none other than Swansea Town. There was no mistake on my part.

'I'd like to buy this one, how much is it?' I asked Derek, trying to keep the excitement from my voice and hoping he wouldn't look at it too closely.

He smiled and said, 'To you, threepence.'

I suddenly felt guilty about what I was doing. 'Are you sure you don't want more than that?'

'No, threepence is fine.'

I handed over the money. I wasn't planning to keep all the proceeds. My plan was to buy myself a Bromley season ticket for ten shillings and a new bike. After that I ran out of ideas, so I decided to give the rest to Bromley, who could spend it in any way they wanted, although a new tea hut might be a good idea. I even allowed myself to drift off into a fantasy about the building of a new Dave Roberts Stand.

Putting the rest of the programmes out took longer than usual that day as I was looking closely at each one for signs of another misprint. There weren't any, but I did manage to pick up a Bradford City v. Bradford Park Avenue from 1963.

When I got home, still on a high after Bromley had taken a point from much-higher-in-the-table Hitchin, I checked the current *Playfair* football annual, eagerly skipping past Jackie Charlton's World Cup article to the previous season's league tables. And sure enough, there was no mention of any Swansea City, only Swansea Town.

I was desperate to find out what my programme was worth and suddenly had an epiphany. There was only one man who would be able to help me. Not only was he an expert on football, he was also a high-profile supporter of Gillingham, Swansea's opponents that day. His name was Brian Moore, host of *The Big Match*, a programme I was a big fan of and had watched every Sunday since it first came on air three years earlier. He was a pleasant-looking balding man who was always immaculately turned out in jacket (usually powder blue or brown) and tie. Like me, the more excited he got, the higher his voice became, which made me feel that he was as passionate about football as I was. He even had a catchphrase, 'hooked off the line', which, although I used it occasionally, never really caught on.

Brian Moore had such a friendly presence that viewers felt they knew him. I certainly felt that way, and I decided to write him a letter (his address at London Weekend Television was helpfully given on *The Big Match*).

Dear Mr Moore,
I am a big fan of *The Big Match* and watch it every Sunday. I have recently acquired a programme for Swansea Town v. your team Gillingham (24/10/70) which as you know Gillingham unfortunately lost 1-0. It has a serious misprint because instead of Swansea Town they have printed Swansea

City on the front cover. I am wondering if you can tell me
what this programme is worth?
Yours sincerely,
David Roberts (15)

I folded it neatly, put it in an envelope and sealed it. Finding a
stamp wasn't a problem. I had loads of them.

As I walked my sister Miriam's dog to the postbox, I wondered
how busy Brian Moore would be. My theory was that since he
only worked on Sundays with the occasional midweek match to
commentate on, he'd have plenty of time to advise me on what
to do. I felt confident he'd reply. My best friend from school,
Dave, had written to him about the perceived anti-Arsenal bias on
The Big Match (he'd included a graph that showed Spurs had
featured more often) and the letter had been read out on air.

It was just a matter of waiting and being patient.

I kept the programme in the pages of the book I was reading,
Skinhead by Richard Allen ('AGGRO – that's what Joe
Hawkins and his mates were looking for'), which was hidden
under my bed. I didn't mention my big misprint discovery to
anyone at school. I knew that if I did they would somehow con
me into giving it to them, as had happened with my favourite
Tighten Up Volume One record. So I kept it to myself, even
though I was bursting to tell someone.

I'd often remove the programme from its hiding place and
read it through, cover to cover. I was particularly struck by
several things: the clever advert for Merriman and Stephens
Ltd Heating Supplies (Goals? see the Swans. COALS? See
Merriman and Stephens); the fact that Swansea was top of the
road safety league, according to another advert; and the way
the club seemed so ashamed of playing in the Third Division –
it wasn't even mentioned once, not even on the cover or the
'fixtures and results' page.

Every day I cycled home from school that little bit faster than usual, stopping only at the sweet shop. I'd recently started alternating between chocolate and crisps after my mum told me that having chocolate every day was probably the reason I was getting fat. As soon as I got home I'd burst into the kitchen, still out of breath, and frantically search for mail. But, apart from the occasional airmail letter from Lotte, my German penpal and unwitting object of my heartfelt love, there was nothing.

As days turned into weeks, it slowly dawned on me that I might not be getting a reply. I knew he wasn't ill or anything because I saw him on *The Big Match* and he looked fine. Maybe he was just too busy. But deep inside I refused to give up hope. I was confident that I'd be able to rely on Brian Moore.

Sure enough, when I woke up one Saturday morning there was a letter for me on the kitchen table with a London W1 postmark. I eagerly ripped it open and my heart beat even faster when I saw the London Weekend Television header at the top of the letter. I was about to find out the true worth of my most treasured possession.

I sat down and read the letter.

Dear David,
I'm afraid Swansea Town became Swansea City at the
beginning of the season!
Very best wishes,
Brian Moore

This was an unforeseen blow. It seemed that at best the programme might be worth the threepence I'd paid for it. I don't think I had felt such crushing disappointment since the last time I'd watched Bromley lose.

Still, I now had something that was potentially very valuable: a signed letter from Brian Moore. I promptly tucked it between the pages of *Skinhead*, convinced that it would be worth a small fortune. Maybe enough for that Bromley season ticket.

I may have been disappointed but there was no blaming the messenger: Brian Moore went from being an amiable TV presenter to sharing the pedestal occupied by my greatest heroes, like George Best, Denis Law and Adrian Street, the wrestler. And they were about to be joined by an obscure Fourth Division centre-forward.

ALDERSHOT FOOTBALL CLUB

OFFICIAL
PROGRAMME

1/-

SEASON 1970-71

**General Manager and
Secretary:** David Smith.

Team Manager: J. Melia.

Ground and Offices:
Recreation Ground, High Street.
Telephone 20211.

Colours: Shirts : Red with
blue numbers. Shorts : Red.

President: D. Llewellyn
Griffiths, O.B.E.

Directors: J. G. Caesar (Chairman),
F. G. Wiltshire (Vice-Chairman),
S. C. Salter, G. H. Cooper, M.B.E.,
S. R. Hooker, G. C. H. Way,
J. H. Barefoot.

FOOTBALL LEAGUE — Fourth Division
Aldershot v. York City

13th March, 1971

No. 20

5

Aldershot v. York City,
13 March 1971

Paul Aimson (centre forward): Rejoined City last season after service with Bury, Bradford City and Huddersfield Town.

From the official programme

Keith was Dave's friend, who lived around the corner from him on the Biggin Hill air force base. The three of us had formed a band, and we spent our evenings practising in Keith's bedroom as there was never anything else to do. We had an unconventional line-up: Keith played acoustic guitar and Dave and I sang, as we couldn't play any instruments. We had three songs: 'Sitting in My Bedroom', 'Looking Out the Window in My Shirtsleeves' and 'Che's Working for the Capitalists Now'. The inspiration for these songs wasn't hard to find. The first two were self-explanatory, the third was a scathing comment on the exploitation of Che Guevara's image on one of the posters that adorned Keith's wall. The songs all had the same tune, 'Close to You' by The Carpenters, which was the only thing Keith could play.

Keith's other passion was York City. Attached with Blu-tack

above his bed was a small poster of their squad, which looked as though it may have been removed from a programme – a thought that filled me with quiet horror. All but two of the players were smiling for the camera as they posed in their maroon shirts and white shorts, seemingly oblivious to the pouring rain. Rain-soaked slate roofs glistened in the background, and the overcast skies barely provided enough light to make the players, hair plastered across their faces, recognizable.

But there was one player, standing third from right, who stood out as far as Keith was concerned. Paul Aimson was the top scorer and Keith's all-time hero, even though living so far from York he'd never seen him in the flesh. Aimson was not only the main reason why York were vying for promotion into the Third Division, he also held the record for the club's fastest ever goal, after only nine seconds against Torquay.

When Keith suggested a trip to Aldershot that Saturday to see them play York we immediately agreed, despite knowing that the entire journey would be spent listening to The Carpenters on the stereo in Keith's Ford Anglia. It was a small price to pay for finally getting to see Paul Aimson, a hero we now worshipped almost as much as he did. Keith had also insisted that we learn to recite the entire York City team from memory, which we enthusiastically managed to do over the course of several weeks. Technically, this probably counted as being brainwashed, but we didn't care. There wasn't much to do in Biggin Hill.

It was because we were so starved of entertainment that Aldershot v. York City loomed as such an appetizing day out. I arranged to stay over at Dave's so we could all leave early and hopefully see the players arrive in their coach. Band practice that night was ruined by Keith's lack of commitment. He seemed more interested in talking about the game than adding to our stockpile of songs so we left early, disillusioned with the music business.

The next morning, Keith was already parked outside Dave's house when we got up. He wouldn't let us into his car until we'd handed over fifty new pence petrol money, but once we'd paid him we were on our way.

The drive to Aldershot was relatively short, and one of the benefits of our early arrival was having the pick of spaces in the still-empty car park. After Keith had fitted his Krooklok, which would prevent anyone from stealing his falling-to-pieces Anglia, we found the entrance. As it was only 12.15 the news that greeted us was exciting but hardly unexpected: the York City coach hadn't got there yet. We would be able to watch them disembark and enter the ground, alongside the handful of diehards clad in maroon and white scarves who were already milling around in eager anticipation.

An hour later, the coach pulled up right outside the entrance and the driver opened the doors.

'There he is!' shouted Keith, pointing an accusatory finger at a player with a familiar brown mop of hair, parted at the side, and a grim expression.

As he walked past, he came close enough for us to pat him on the back. Keith patted him on the back. 'Hat-trick today, Paul!' he yelled. Dave joined in with a 'Yeah, get a hat-trick, Paul!' and I added an uninspired 'Good luck, Paul.' He looked a bit puzzled, possibly unused to such attention, and went through the gate into the Recreation Ground with his teammates.

Our insistence on greeting the players meant we now had to waste nearly two hours before the game began, but that didn't worry us. We were used to standing around feeling bored, so that was what we did. We stood around inside the ground feeling bored until the players ran out.

The first thing we noticed was that Paul Aimson wasn't taking many shots in the warm-up, and as soon as he removed his tracksuit top the reason became clear. The number 3 on his back tipped us off that the player we had identified as Paul Aimson from the poorly lit photo on Keith's wall was in fact Phil Burrows.

This case of mistaken identity was soon forgotten as the game got underway. Unfortunately, we couldn't offer York any vocal support due to the presence of a large contingent of squaddies from the local army bases, who wore red and blue scarves. There didn't seem to be any sense in provoking them, so we agreed on a strategy of quietly praising any moments of York or Aimson magic between ourselves.

In the event, there weren't any. It was the worst half of football I'd ever seen, and that included Orpington and Bromley District Sunday League games in the park. Skill levels were on a par with my school team. There was only one shot on target in the whole of the opening forty-five minutes, which York keeper Ron Hillyard comfortably saved. Paul Aimson had been a totally anonymous figure, as had all the others whose names we had committed to memory. Our illusions were well on the way to being shattered.

I'd been so stunned by the mediocrity that I'd even forgotten to read the programme. When I did, two things stood out. First, the sheer awfulness of Aldershot's reserve team, who were having a terrible season – two wins in thirty-odd games, with a constant string of five- and six-goal defeats. It took me back to Bromley's similar performances the previous season. But of even more interest was a small article headed CALLING ALL SUPPORTERS, which I had to read twice to make sure I wasn't imagining it. That night, after the match, they were holding the Annual Beauty Queen Competition and Dance at the Civic Hall in Camberley.

Now, Keith, Dave and I were all single. That's what tends to happen when you spend your entire lives outside school in your mate's bedroom or on the terraces of lower league football grounds. And, suddenly, we had the chance to meet 'fifteen attractive girls' who would be 'competing for the top prizes and the right to represent Aldershot Supporters' Club in the Southern Area finals later in the year'. *Fifteen* attractive girls. Who liked football. This was the greatest opportunity of our lives. Even if ten of them didn't fancy us, we'd still have a chance of getting a girlfriend. The odds were heavily in our favour.

Or they would have been had Keith not spotted something I'd missed in my enthusiasm to share the news. I'd read the bit that said 'Dress is optional' and was satisfied that we'd get in wearing a fake sheepskin jacket (me) and denim jackets (Dave and Keith). Unfortunately, the full sentence read: 'Dress is optional – evening or lounge suits – but ties must be worn, otherwise admission will be refused.'

My heart sank. It looked like being another Saturday night spent in Keith's bedroom, writing a load of songs that all sounded exactly the same. The day was turning out to be even more bleak and miserable than usual.

But then, after seventy-odd minutes, everything changed. Paul Aimson, shaking himself out of his stupor, made a run towards the Aldershot goal. He was brought down by a clumsy challenge and the referee, as he had spent most of the match doing, blew his whistle officiously. Mackin floated the free kick into the box and Chris Topping ran between two defenders to head the ball over the advancing Dixon.

Suddenly, all was right with the world. It was now a great game and the mighty York were heading for a thrilling and well-deserved win which could take them into sixth place. Jimmy Melia, the Aldershot player/manager, immediately took himself off, but this tactical ploy made no difference and York City, *our* York City, held on.

Due to the presence of the squaddies, we had to contain our

joy until we were safely back in Keith's Anglia, where talk turned to how we were going to celebrate the brilliant win. We were just outside Guildford when inspiration struck me like a bolt of lightning. We'd been talking about football songs like the England team's 'Back Home' and thought it would be great if York had one, now that they were our team. The thinking was that it would not only help them, but also be good for the band, especially if we could release it as a single under the alias of The Minster Men, which was York's nickname.

When we got back to Keith's, Dave and I sat on the floor, hunched over an exercise book, writing and rewriting lyrics, while Keith strummed the familiar chords of 'Close to You'. We occasionally glanced up at the wall, seeking inspiration from the team photo. We wanted to write an anthem, one that could be sung on the terraces and that celebrated the genius of Paul Aimson and as many others as we could fit in. Eventually, after much crossing out and disagreement, we arrived at some lyrics we all felt were perfect. We were ready to lay the track down on tape.

As it was Dave's cassette recorder, he designated himself producer in addition to his singing duties, so he counted down and then pressed Play and Record. On his nod, Keith launched into the intro, than Dave and I started singing more self-consciously than usual, aware that others would be listening to the tape. I also had a slight suspicion that the lyrics might not be quite as good as we'd convinced ourselves they were. But I still put everything into my performance.

On the day that Paul was born, the angels got together, and decided to create a team so good,
So they gave Ron Hillyard the goalie's gloves, then they
    picked young Chris Topping, too (do–do–do, do–do–do).
That is why football fans in town

Follow you all around.
Just like me, they long to see, York Ci-ty.

On about the eighth take, Dave pronounced himself happy. 'It's a wrap' were his exact words, and we played it back over and over again, thrilled with the result.

In our dinner break the following Monday, Dave and I sneaked out of school and up the road to Elmers End Post Office, where we posted the tape to Tom Johnston, The Manager, York City, Bootham Crescent, York, Yorkshire. The rest of the day was spent imagining the players sitting around in the dressing room singing along to it. We even entertained thoughts about Phil Burrows proudly leading the team on to the field with our song playing over the Tannoy. We went around school singing the song to ourselves, totally convinced it would be on Radio One in a few weeks' time, although we were realistic enough to know that we might have to re-record it.

But our song was to prove yet another in an endless line of teenage disappointments. We never did hear back from York City and the band split up shortly after, when I left citing 'musical differences'. Seduced by the skinhead lifestyle, I was now listening exclusively to reggae and Tamla Motown. Skinheads and The Carpenters didn't really go together, and I desperately wanted to be a skinhead.

Football League—Division One

FOREST REVIEW

OFFICIAL MATCH DAY MAGAZINE   FIVE NEW PENCE

Nottingham Forest   Arsenal

TUESDAY, 13th APRIL, 1971   Kick-off 7.30 p.m.

6

Nottingham Forest v. Arsenal,
13 April 1971

Someone once said that football is a funny game but unfortunately there has been little fun for those teams struggling in the relegation zone. The 1970/71 campaign has been one full of worries and strains as far as we are concerned.

From the official programme

The far corner of the school playground was considered a no-go zone during the dinner hour. It was the exclusive territory of four or five Arsenal-supporting skinheads, who had achieved notoriety in the national press for football hooliganism. Other pupils, especially those with a fully functional survival instinct, stayed well clear. Not me. I was desperate to be accepted by them, despite being among the least threatening boys in the entire school and never having had a fight in my life. For some unknown reason, one of them seemed to quite like me, a sign that I had begun to misinterpret as meaning I could hang out with him and his fellow celebrity thugs in the playground.

Chewing a piece of imaginary gum, I approached him, nodding a curt greeting in the way I'd seen them do to each other.

'Orright?' I said, in an attempt at a deep, gruff voice.

'Orright,' he replied in an effortlessly genuine deep, gruff voice.

Struggling for a follow-up to my greeting, I was inspired by the sight of the red and white scarf knotted around his left wrist.

'Going to Forest tonight?' I asked. Arsenal were playing there in a game that was crucial for their title hopes, so I assumed he'd be there.

He looked at me, a sudden spark of interest in his eyes. 'Nah,' he eventually replied. 'You?'

'Yeah,' I said with feigned nonchalance.

The truth was, I had no intention of going. I would simply read the match report in the next morning's *Guardian* and then describe events as though I'd been there. This plan was thrown into disarray by his response.

'Get us a programme, then.'

It wasn't a request, it was a demand. As the seriousness of the situation started to sink in, I felt a wave of panic rise inside me. This was catastrophic on many different levels. I wasn't an Arsenal fan, although I'd been trying to give the impression that I was. I was also broke and planning on an evening in watching TV. But there was no way out now.

By the time the bell went for the end of school I'd been asked to get programmes for four different people, including my best friend Dave. I'd begged him to come with me, but he couldn't as he had to study.

I cycled home in a state of high anxiety, knowing that I some-how had to find at least three pounds and then get to St Pancras in just over an hour for the 16.50 train to Nottingham. I didn't want to catch the Football Special, as that would be packed with skinheads and I was fairly certain I'd get beaten up as they were bound to expose me for only pretending to be an Arsenal fan. Being as non-specific as possible, I told my mum I was 'off to the match'. She was used to me leaving ages before kick-off as I liked to watch the players getting off the coach, so probably didn't suspect that I was going half the length of the country to buy half a dozen programmes.

After stopping off at the post office to remove the last of my savings from my paper round, I got to St Pancras with time to spare. The two-and-a-half-hour train journey gave me plenty of time to reflect on what it was that was making me so desperate to get in with the skinheads. I suspected that reading Richard Allen's *Skinhead* series was at least partly responsible, as it made it sound very glamorous and Joe Hawkins, the main character in the books, was well liked and always got plenty of 'sorts', which was what he called girls. It was also a shortcut to popularity, as everyone was either scared of them or just in awe.

Having been so anxious about being forced to go to Nottingham, I'd been too nervous to eat lunch at school, so I took my sandwiches from my Adidas bag and ate them on the train. I was pleased with myself for saving money – British Rail sandwiches were notoriously expensive – so, to celebrate my financial acumen, I treated myself to a cup of coffee.

I tried to look on the bright side of my involuntary trip to Nottingham. It would definitely boost my reputation at school, and I might even enjoy it. In fact, I was quite excited about the match. Not as excited as I would have been if Bromley were playing, but definitely looking forward to it. There would be some big names playing, such as Storey-Moore for Forest and Wilson, Rice, McNab, Storey, McLintock, Simpson, Armstrong, Graham, Radford, Kennedy and George for Arsenal. And, after all, if you're going to start supporting a high-profile team, it's easier if you pick a winning one. Arsenal were in with a good chance of the league and FA Cup double.

There were literally thousands of Arsenal fans milling around the station when I got off and I somehow found myself pushed in with them. We were given a police escort to the City Ground – something I couldn't wait to tell everyone about the next day. When we got there, I bought half a dozen extra programmes and placed them carefully in my now-empty sandwich box, which I then put in my bag. Having committed myself to a six-hour round trip to get them, I thought I might as well get a few spares. There was a big crowd and the Arsenal fans were herded into the Bridgford Stand behind the goal. I made sure I was standing as far away as possible from the obvious troublemakers.

As I was reading the programme, I was surprised to hear the Forest fans at the opposite end singing one of my favourite songs, 'Wanderin' Star' by Lee Marvin, although they'd adapted the words to 'I was born under a Trent End goal', which didn't appear to make any sense. The Arsenal fans seemed in good spirits, too. A win tonight would put them within two points of league leaders Leeds with two games in hand and there was a real feeling of excitement all around me.

The match started dramatically with Forest almost scoring in the very first minute, when Neil Martin took on the defence. Only Bob Wilson's bravery in diving at his feet kept the game scoreless. A quarter of an hour later Ray Kennedy, who had got a hat-trick when the sides met earlier in the season, continued his one-man vendetta against Forest by tapping in following a goalmouth scramble. It looked to me as though Frank McLintock's header had already crossed the line, but the ground announcer gave the goal to Kennedy.

Arsenal never really looked like champions in waiting, but they were just about doing enough to win. Their second goal came about ten minutes before half time when Kennedy headed in from a George Graham flick, and the contest was effectively over.

Although I did have a passing interest in the game, it wasn't enough to stop me leaving as soon as Kennedy's second goal went in, as I wanted to be sure of getting the 20.19, which was the last train back to London. At 2–0 up it was clear Arsenal were going to win and I'd seen enough to be able to talk convincingly about the game in the playground the next day.

As I left the ground, I decided to take a shortcut along the riverbank to the bridge that would get me on to London Road, which led to the station. I scoured the river for the old man who spent the whole of every match rowing around in a coracle, collecting stray footballs that had been kicked from the ground and returning them, but stopped looking when I remembered he was in Shrewsbury, not Nottingham.

As I was jogging past a couple of trees on the riverbank, I was suddenly stopped by a small group of Forest supporters who, I belatedly realized, were lying in wait for visiting fans.

'Where are you from?' said one of them, in a not altogether friendly way.

Despite being terrified, I knew I had to try and stay calm and convince them I was a local. 'Nottingham,' I replied, attempting to mimic his accent. Unfortunately I sounded more like Blakey from the ITV sitcom *On the Buses*.

'What school d'you go to, then?' he said, apparently not convinced.

The panic was rising inside me. Should I say something like Nottingham Grammar? Or Nottingham School? In hindsight, anything would have been better than what I came out with.

'I dunno, I've forgotten,' I stammered desperately.

And then I started running as fast as I could in the direction of the bridge. I knew that if they managed to catch me I'd either be (a) beaten up or (b) thrown into the Trent, neither of which was preferable to the other. As I glanced over my shoulder (which our PE teacher had told us never to do in a race), I saw that the distance between us was increasing slightly. Doc Martens weren't really made for running and that was probably what saved me. I ran and ran and didn't stop running until I arrived, totally exhausted and dripping with sweat, at the station. The train was waiting and I clambered on board, looking anxiously out of the window in case they were still after me. It was only a minute or so before we pulled away and I could relax.

It was at least ten more minutes before I stopped gasping for air, and another ten minutes after that for my sides to stop hurting. Ironically, because my watch was slow, I might well have missed the train if I hadn't been chased.

Once I'd got my breath back, I put my programme face down on the table and tried to have a nap, but couldn't as I was too excited. I went to the buffet car and got a cup of coffee and a packet of twenty Number Six, instead of my usual Benson and Hedges. I had no idea why I'd done this; perhaps I'd just fancied a change. Back in my seat sipping the steaming hot coffee, I realized just how impressionable I was: on the back of the programme was an advert that said PLAYERS NO. 6 GIVE YOU GUARANTEED QUALITY and showed a couple of packs identical to the one I'd just bought.

I spent virtually the entire journey reading and re-reading the programme, and by the time we pulled into St Pancras I was convinced I knew the contents off by heart. The only regret I had about leaving Nottingham was that I'd miss the Forest v. Notts County testimonial match for Alan Hill, which was advertised in the programme and promised a 'Hot Pants' Queen Contest. At least I wouldn't have to endure the marching band, which had thoughtfully been lined up. I got a small feeling of satisfaction from imagining the skinheads having to sit through it. Perfect revenge for what they'd put me through.

When I finally got home, everyone was asleep. I didn't get to bed until long after midnight, yet couldn't wait to get to school the next day and tell everyone about the game. I'd already decided to leave out the bit about being chased along the riverbank as I felt that might threaten my newfound football hardman status.

The next morning I dragged myself out of bed, looking forward to handing over the programmes. I packed them away in my Adidas bag and sat down for my traditional breakfast of Marmite on buttered Weetabix, the newspaper spread out in front of me. To my immense satisfaction, I discovered that I'd only missed a late goal from Charlie George in a fairly dull second half. I'd been there for most of the important action.

I avoided the skinheads until the dinner break, as I wanted the handover to take place in the playground, in front of as many people as possible. As I sauntered over to their corner, the one responsible for my Nottingham trip left his conversation to come and talk to me.

'Cheers,' he said as I casually handed him his programme, dismissing his offer of five pence with a raised palm and a 'nah don't worry bardit'.

'Good game?' he asked.

'Yeah, not bad,' I replied, in the slightly bored tone of someone who witnesses dozens of such games every season. I described the highlights in detail, although when I said the bit about Charlie George 'imperiously sweeping the ball into the net' for the third goal I realized this was a direct quote from the paper and a bit of a giveaway that I hadn't seen it. Luckily, he was unlikely to be a *Guardian* reader.

It was a novel feeling to have skinheads approaching me and talking, instead of the other way round. As I distributed the programmes I was really enjoying basking in their attention, especially as I suspected none of them had believed I'd actually go to Nottingham. Arsenal's stock had never been higher at school, and I was benefiting. They had become odds-on favourites for the title, especially with a game against Burnley, who were on their way to the Second Division, only a week away.

This would turn out to be a fixture that humiliated me so much that I would never be able to go to Highbury again.

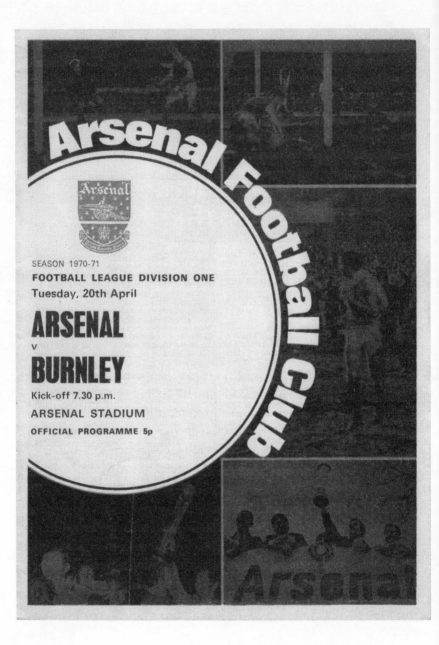

SEASON 1970-71

FOOTBALL LEAGUE DIVISION ONE

Tuesday, 20th April

ARSENAL

v

BURNLEY

Kick-off 7.30 p.m.

ARSENAL STADIUM

OFFICIAL PROGRAMME 5p

7

Arsenal v. Burnley,
20 April 1971

Top of the league – 8 wins in the last 8 league games and 15
goals against one – a great tribute to the skill and enthusiasm of
the whole team – we hope you will drive them on this evening
by your enthusiasm.

From the official programme

I had been off school for the best part of the week with a cold
and had got thoroughly used to the lifestyle. Lying in bed with
bottles of Lucozade to keep my strength up, peanuts to snack
on, and Ribena and aspirin to keep the fever at bay seemed
infinitely preferable to double maths, chemistry and biology.
And to make sure I had even less motivation to recover, my
parents had moved their colour TV into my room, and brought
me the *Guardian* every morning when they'd finished with it.

I would have been happy to stay like this for ever, if it hadn't
been for the lure of football. Although Bromley didn't have a
game, I'd agreed to go to Highbury with Dave to see his
beloved Gunners in action against Burnley, despite what was,
in truth, a mild cold. The added bonus was that most of the

skinheads from school would be there and my credibility with them was at an all-time high following my programme-buying excursion to Nottingham on their behalf the previous Tuesday.

Tonight's game had taken on added significance following what had happened at the Leeds v. WBA match on the Saturday. Leeds had needed a win to stay two points ahead of Arsenal but had gone a goal down early on before one of the most bizarre incidents I'd ever seen on a football pitch took place. I'd watched it unfold on *Match of the Day* and shared commentator Barry Davies' astonishment from the comfort of my sickbed. A misplaced pass from Norman Hunter had hit Tony Brown, the Albion striker, and rebounded into the Leeds half, where Albion's Colin Suggett was standing around twenty yards offside. The linesman dutifully raised his flag and Brown slowed to a stroll as he waited for the inevitable whistle. It didn't come. 'The referee's waving him on!' screeched Davies in disbelief, the injustice he was feeling clear for all to hear. 'Brown is going straight through . . . taking on Sprake!' Davies then temporarily lost the power of speech as Brown passed across the face of the goal to Jeff Astle, who put the ball into the unguarded net. 'And the goal to Astle!' he finally sputtered as a sheepish-looking Astle raised his arm in triumph.

Davies wasn't going to sit on the fence with this one. 'And Leeds will go mad,' he shouted, 'and they've every right to go mad because everybody stopped with the linesman's flag.' And go mad they did. The players surrounded the referee, Ray Tinkler, pleading with him to change his mind. Manager Don Revie, in his trademark blue gaberdine coat, rushed on to the pitch, inexplicably clutching a tartan blanket. And a heavily whiskered Leeds fan in a mustard-coloured Burton's blazer with blue tie was grabbed by two burly policemen before he could inflict any damage on Mr Tinkler.

The protests were to no avail and Leeds eventually lost 2–1.

This meant that if Arsenal could beat Burnley tonight, they would almost certainly win the title. I was desperate to go, but despite my best efforts to explain, my parents didn't seem to grasp the distinction between being too ill to go to school and not being too ill to go and watch football. The only way they'd let me go was if I promised to go back to school the next day. In a bizarre twist, instead of pretending to be ill, which was something I'd done on so many occasions that I'd lost count, I'd have to pretend to be well. After announcing my miraculous recovery, I phoned Dave and arranged to meet him at Bromley South station after tea.

As soon as I saw him, my feeling of general unwellness was replaced by one of resentful envy. He was wearing a purple and black Budgie Jacket – the same one I'd had my eye on since we'd seen it in the window of Top Man a couple of weeks earlier. I knew the faux suede would make him irresistible to sorts, while I was stuck with wearing the faux sheepskin I'd got for Christmas a year and a half ago, back when they were fashionable.

I sulked for most of the train journey, but my spirits started to lift as we approached Highbury, despite coughing a lot and suffering from a mild headache. Dave diagnosed me as having 'caught exposure', which I wasn't convinced about. He had to lend me the forty pence (we were still struggling to get used to decimal currency) to get into the ground as I'd already spent my pocket money. I had no intention of paying him back.

We went to what we called 'our usual place' in the North Bank, even though we'd only been there once before, and found a good spot near the front. My cough was getting worse, so I put a Victory V lozenge in my mouth to stop the irritation in my throat. They were so hot and fiery that only North Bank hardmen like me could put up with the chloroform and ether taste without spitting them out.

Trying to ignore the burning sensation on my near-numb tongue, I glanced through the programme. The only major absences from the Arsenal team were Peter Storey (mysteriously dubbed 'the fridge kid of this jet aged soccer' in that morning's paper) and Bob McNab, who had both been called into the England squad for their game the following evening against Greece.

Suddenly, a familiar voice came over the Tannoy. It was Arsenal's manager Bertie Mee, urging the fans to make themselves heard on this crucial night for their title chances. 'We need more vocal support,' he pleaded. This wasn't really what someone with an agonizing sore throat wanted to hear, but the fans responded by bursting into song. To the tune of 'Rule Britannia', 'Good old Arsenal, we're proud to say that name, and while we sing this song we'll win the game' was repeated over and over again, as those were apparently the only words the song had. On the plus side, it didn't take me long to learn it. The lyrics, Dave informed me, had been written by Jimmy Hill after he'd held a contest on *The Big Match* to compose a song for Arsenal and couldn't find a winner since all the entries had been rubbish.

As the sole verse was being sung for about the fiftieth time, the players appeared and Burnley's albino goalkeeper, the ever-smiling Peter Mellor, ran out in front of the North Bank. We gave him a huge ovation, which he acknowledged gratefully. It was his first league game for four months and he couldn't have picked a bigger one for his comeback. If Burnley lost, they'd be relegated.

After twenty minutes of not much happening, during which time I got through about five Victory Vs, Mellor gave a fair indication of why he'd spent so long out of the first team. He went to catch a John Radford long throw and fell over, leaving Ray Kennedy to head the ball in the direction of the goal. Left winger Eric Probert made a diving save, tipping the ball away with his hand, and the penalty was duly awarded by the referee, Mr T. W. Dawes (Norwich).

I looked around for penalty king Peter Storey, then remembered he was on England duty. Charlie George, whose every touch was greeted with frenzied shrieking from Dave, stepped forward, sent Mellor the wrong way and it was 1–0. The goal seemed to release Arsenal's tension and they started to play the way I'd seen so often that season on TV. I was really starting to enjoy watching an outstanding team at the top of their game.

Then my legs gave way and everything went black.

The next thing I was aware of was an intense bright light and the sound of trumpets. Was I in heaven? No, I was lying on a bed, and a St John Ambulance man who bore a strong resemblance to the actor Oliver Reed was peering intently at my face and shining a torch into my eyes.

'Where am I?' I asked groggily.

'You're in the first-aid room at the Arsenal,' he explained, before adding, somewhat unnecessarily, 'you fainted.'

I wanted to go back out, but he wouldn't let me, insisting I stay there and drink a cup of sweet tea first. If there are two tastes that don't mix, it's tea and Victory V residue, but since it was the only way I'd be able to get back to the football, I gulped it down.

He then escorted me down the corridor, where I finally discovered why I'd heard trumpets. The brass band were warming up for their half-time display and were running through a selection of songs from *Mary Poppins*. We walked past them and out on to the cinder track surrounding the pitch. A glance at the giant clock at the aptly named Clock End confirmed that there were still a few minutes left of the first half. The scoreboard showed an unchanged scoreline: Arsenal were still one up.

It was a thrill being so close to the players and I walked as slowly as possible to make the most of the opportunity, even though I felt everyone was watching me. When the Oliver Reed lookalike opened the gate and let me back into the North Bank, I thanked him and then scoured the packed stand for a shortish, slim, long-haired figure in a Budgie Jacket. Despite spotting dozens, none of them was Dave.

I watched the second half on my own. Burnley looked like a team resigned to relegation and Arsenal were by far the better side, without really threatening to add to their solitary goal. But to the North Bank, the score was irrelevant. The two points were all that mattered, and the roar that greeted the final whistle signified that they knew the title was now within reach.

When I got home, I immediately rang Dave to find out what had happened. According to him, he was talking to me while he was watching the game. When I didn't say anything, he turned round to demand a reply and I wasn't there. Someone nudged him and pointed to a couple of St John Ambulance men carrying me round the hallowed turf (as he called it) on a stretcher. He had no interest in finding out if I was feeling any better, but was desperate to find out what it was like under the East Stand.

It didn't take long to get to sleep that night and I woke the next morning with my throat no longer sore, which I attributed to the Victory Vs. After breakfast and a quick read of the *Guardian*, where I learned that George Best had once again gone missing from the Northern Ireland squad, I bravely went to school, confident that this would prove how hard I was.

The playground had already been the site of one of my most humiliating moments, when I attempted the Willie Carr free kick in front of dozens of people. The idea was to grip the ball between the ankles and flick it up in the air for the person standing behind to volley. This was what had happened when Coventry played Everton earlier in the season, Carr and Ernie

Hunt combining for one of the goals of the season. What happened when I tried it was that the ball remained on the ground and I managed to kick myself ferociously in the nads with both heels, before collapsing in a screaming heap.

And now that same playground was about to be the scene of something even more embarrassing.

As I walked into it the day after the Burnley match, I didn't quite get the hero's reception I'd been anticipating. Instead, one after the other, the skinheads (including the one I thought liked me) collapsed to the ground laughing, pretending to faint. This then spread to several other boys, who took their turns to fall to the ground. The humiliation rose inside me, but I was determined not to show them how devastated I was.

It was clear that my skinhead days were over, but football showed no sign of loosening the grip it had on me. I was spending more and more time at Hayes Lane, home of Bromley, a team that won about as frequently as Arsenal lost. Expectations were always low – until one perfect day that autumn.

Official Programme 3p
Ground : HAYES LANE
BROMLEY, KENT
Phone : 460 5291

Season 1971/72
Hon Sec. : Mr. C. F. KING
"Rosings", Falcon Avenue,
Bickley, Kent. 460-4750

Bromley Football Club

**MEMBERS OF THE F.A., L.F.A., K.C.F.A. and ISTHMIAN LEAGUE
FOUNDED 1892**

Past Successes—Winners of Amateur Cup (three times); London Senior Cup
(three times); Kent Senior Cup; Kent Amateur Cup (twelve times); S.L. Charity
Cup; Bromley Hospital Cup (fifteen times); Athenian League (three times);
Isthmian League (four times); London League; Spartan League; S.E. Combination;
Athenian League Reserves Section (four times); Athenian League Reserves
Challenge Cup (twice); South Thames Challenge Cup; London Intermediate Cup.
Kent Floodlight Cup (Western Section) Winners.

8

Bromley v. Civil Service,
18 September 1971

We have, for some time past, been subjected to some rowdyism caused by a group of youngsters who seem to have little or no interest in watching the game being played. We would give these youngsters this final warning, that if they do not cease this unrulyness, which includes the use of foul language, we shall ban all youngsters from our ground who are not attended by adults.

From the official programme

At sixteen, on the verge of adulthood, a glorious constellation of factors had come together to conjure up a fixture that looked like producing the kind of outcome I'd dreamed about since I'd first watched Bromley. The novel experience of a big win looked a distinct possibility, which would help wipe out the memories of the many huge defeats I'd forced myself to sit through.

Although Bromley had provided me with the majority of the disappointments I'd suffered so far in life, my optimism, for once, looked justified. In the FA Cup first qualifying round they had been drawn to play the Civil Service, a team who were so useless they weren't even meant to be in the FA Cup and had only been invited to take part because it was their centenary year. They were basically a park side who played in the Southern Amateur League, a lowly league that was only a few levels up from the one I played in on Sundays. Bromley, however, were in the far superior Isthmian League and were having a pretty good season, if you discounted the fact that they were second from bottom of the table and had scored in only one of their last six games.

The Civil Service had originally been drawn at home, but since home was a park, the game was transferred to Hayes Lane. In the highly unlikely case of a replay, this would also take place at Hayes Lane.

There was another factor that made the whole thing seem lopsided. Bromley's massive new signing, Welsh amateur international Tony Nantcurvis, had been cleared to play thanks to some fancy footwork by Bromley chairman Charlie King. He'd been on holiday in South Wales and had taken the opportunity to contact the Llanelli manager about Nantcurvis, who had shown up at Hayes Lane asking for a trial. After being assured of the player's undoubted quality, Mr King then lobbied the FA Hardship Committee and had got permission to play him in the match.

We also had superstar centre-forward Jim Brown, who had filled the gaping void in my life left by Alan Stonebridge, my previous hero. Stonebridge had gone off to Carshalton midway through the 1969/70 season, the worst in the club's history, and it still hurt to think about it. But Brown was so good that manager Alan Basham had been forced to tear up his book of tactics and use just one up front. Jim Brown would stand just inside his own half and someone, usually Roy Pettet, would hoof the ball forward. Brown's exceptional speed meant that he would easily outsprint the defence and, more often than not, calmly score yet another goal.

As I approached the ground on my new second-hand scooter, with DAVE BROMLEY clumsily fashioned from masking tape on the windshield, I found myself relishing the imminent goalfest. I paid my ten pence (the price had doubled six months earlier, when I turned sixteen) and entered the ground, where I bought a Golden Goal ticket from Roy, a fellow member of the supporters club and companion on many away trips.

My old friend The Grubby was waiting for me on the far side, his long ginger locks making him easy to pick out in a crowd and even easier to pick out when there was no crowd, which seemed to be the case today. Perhaps the Civil Service weren't a big draw, or perhaps everyone saw the game as a fore-gone conclusion.

It almost seemed unfair, and The Grubby and I probably would have felt sorry for the Civil Service if we hadn't hated them so much. We wanted to see them crushed and humiliated, the reason being that we had recently left school and we both now worked for the Civil Service. We were resentful and bitter employees, sulkily handing our souls over to bureaucrats between nine and five every day. I had to make tea and photo-copies at Somerset House, while The Grubby had to interview Bromley's vast army of unemployed at the local dole office. We saw this game as an opportunity for redemption, with Bromley FC striking a blow on our behalf.

As a gesture designed to show how much we believed in our team, we decided to watch this vital game from behind the opposition's goal. Under normal circumstances this would have been a futile exercise, leaving us squinting into the distance, trying to make out the action, but surely Bromley wouldn't let us down this time.

As the teams ran out, I couldn't help but notice that the Civil

Service players all *looked* like civil servants. Not in the sense that they wore suits and bowler hats and carried umbrellas, but because they had about them a grey air of resignation combined with earnest endeavour, which The Grubby and I instantly recognized from our work colleagues, and were starting to see in ourselves.

One of the benefits of standing behind the goal that Bromley were attacking was the proximity of the tea hut. I usually worked in it, which meant that I spent both work and leisure time making tea, despite not being particularly good at it. But today, thanks to severe public lack of interest in the fixture, I wasn't needed. The Grubby ensured that they had at least one customer by buying four cups of heavily sugared tea for us, which I petulantly felt was inferior to the usual brew.

The game kicked off, and after five minutes our moods had darkened. Bromley hadn't scored. They hadn't even threatened to score. Why could other teams hammer Bromley, but Bromley couldn't hammer other teams? It didn't seem right.

The Grubby was already on to his second Benson and Hedges of the day and was threatening to go home and watch the racing on TV, as that would be more interesting. He must have been seriously disillusioned with Bromley's early efforts, because The Grubby hated racing.

Luckily our impatience was rewarded just four minutes later, when Ray Hutchins went on a run, crossed the ball and, right in front of us, Jim Brown calmly tucked the ball past the goalkeeper. The second followed a few minutes later, when Brown went on one of his sprints from the halfway line and pulled the ball back to Tony Coppin, who, when he finally caught up, made it 2–0.

The lukewarm tea was tasting like champagne after fourteen minutes, when Brown's outrageous overhead kick put the home side 3–0 up. This was payback for all those heavy defeats. This was payback for all those long hours photocopying reports so dreary that surely no one would ever read them.

Ten minutes after that, Tony Nantcurvis, the Welsh wizard (as I had inevitably dubbed him), took centre stage, scurrying down the right and putting in a perfect cross which Coppin headed against the bar, even though it would have been easier to score. The angst lasted only a split second, as John Campbell blasted the rebound into the net for Bromley's fourth. It was technically offside, according to Law 11 in the *FA Rule Book*, which my dad had bought me after the Fulham v. Manchester United game seven years earlier, but the referee didn't seem to notice. He was probably still admiring the Nantcurvis run.

Coppin's moment of redemption wasn't long in coming. He put away a far harder chance to make it five, and the sixth goal came when Jim Brown made his traditional sprint from halfway to finish with ease and earn himself a first-half hat-trick. It wasn't even half time and Bromley were 6–0 up. The Grubby and I stared at each other, our eyes ablaze with emotion. 'Six nil!' we repeated over and over again, as though we couldn't quite believe our eyes. Bromley 6 Someone Else 0. Neither of us had experienced anything like it.

We were getting greedy now, deciding that double figures was the least we expected. I was hoping for fifteen, The Grubby was more ambitious, feeling that a twenty-goal margin was the minimum amount he would settle for, including fourteen from Jim Brown.

The Civil Service's half-time talk was obviously rubbish, as Bromley's seventh and Jim Brown's fourth came just minutes after the restart, following some embarrassingly easy dribbling from Hutchins. I was starting to feel a bit faint with all the excitement and had to run over to the tea hut for a four-heaped-teaspoons-of-sugar cup of tea. The Grubby had the same, not for medical reasons, but because that was what he always had.

Before the tea had had a chance to cool down, it was 8–0. Roy Pettet's magnificent pass, wasted on that day's opponents, was converted by Campbell.

After this goal I noticed that the Bromley players had become reluctant to pass, preferring to go for glory themselves. This threatened to slow the scoring down, but not for long. Jim Brown's solo effort (I had a feeling all the goals from now on were going to be solo efforts) gave him a total of five and the team a total of nine. And when Roy Pettet's goal-bound shot was un-necessarily poked over the line by Campbell for his hat-trick, Bromley had reached double figures.

And there was still over a quarter of an hour left. Enough time for Bromley to miss countless chances, half chances, and even a couple of open goals.

Usually when watching Bromley I couldn't wait for the final whistle. Today, hearing it was a huge disappointment. Still, Bromley had not only scored ten goals, they'd also dominated a game from start to finish. I now knew how supporters of most of Bromley's opponents felt.

It just went to show. If you wait long enough for something good to happen and you don't lose faith, your time will eventually come. Even if it is against a really useless team.

Going to work on Monday morning was going to be a little less soul-destroying than usual. And every time something went wrong at work, I knew I'd be able to think back on what I'd just witnessed and smile inwardly.

But that wasn't the last time football and the Civil Service would face each other on a collision course. The next occasion had a far less predictable outcome.

HAMMER

THE OFFICIAL PROGRAMME OF
WEST HAM UNITED

HEREFORD UNITED

FOOTBALL ASSOCIATION CUP : Fourth Round replay

Monday 14 February 1972 at 2.15 p.m.

FIVEPENCE

36

9

West Ham United v. Hereford United,
14 February 1972

In the circumstances we decided that for technical reasons it would be safer to ensure a 16-page production on this occasion instead of our normal 20 pages.

From the official programme

It was Valentine's Day in 1972, and non-league Hereford United were the most famous football team in England. They'd just knocked mighty Newcastle United out of the FA Cup in probably the biggest shock of all time, and then held West Ham to a 0–0 draw at their Edgar Street ground in the next round. In just a few hours' time the replay would be taking place at West Ham's Upton Park.

I desperately wanted to be there, but instead I was sitting at my desk at the Principal Probate Registry (Family Division). It was the only one of the seven desks in the room without a Valentine's card on it. Instead I had a mountain of files piled up in front of me, and was slowly working through them – the picture of a conscientious civil servant. But my mind was elsewhere, specifically Edgar Street nine days earlier. I was reliving

Ronnie Radford's incredible goal from thirty yards out against Newcastle over and over again, hearing commentator John Motson's boyish delight as he screamed, 'Oh, what a goal – *what* a goal! Radford the scorer! Ronnie Radford!'

Would Radford, a carpenter by trade, manage another screamer against West Ham today? Could Hereford once again upset one of the country's leading teams? While these questions were being answered, I would be sitting in a freezing cold office alongside six shivering civil servants, filing and photocopying. Tasks that are made harder when you have thick woollen mittens on your hands to keep them warm.

Like everyone else, I was wearing gloves as well as my duffel coat and scarf because of the coal miners' strike, which meant power cuts everywhere. It wasn't just the lack of heating and lighting that upset me and my colleagues, it was the lack of tea-making facilities that really hurt, and this had prompted someone to bring in a small camping stove. The absence of electricity was why the replay was taking place at 2.15 on a Monday afternoon. West Ham wouldn't be able to use their floodlights.

Hereford had captured the public's imagination and were providing a welcome distraction from the discomfort stemming from the strikes. An Australian millionaire had even made an optimistic bid for the club with the intention of importing them lock, stock and barrel to Sydney. The point of this wasn't entirely clear, but it did sum up the fascination people had for them, myself included.

I wasn't a terribly convincing Hereford fan, but when you support Bromley, you tend automatically to empathize with the underdog. I wasn't even totally certain what country Hereford was in. I thought it might be Wales. Or possibly England. I also only knew the names of three of their team: Radford and Ricky George, both of whom had scored against Newcastle, and goalkeeper Fred Potter, usually described as 'resolute' in the paper.

Just thinking about these players made me decide to make one last, desperate attempt to get the afternoon off so I could go to Upton Park. I had put in an application for half a day's leave the previous Thursday, as soon as the replay date was announced. Unsurprisingly, it had been returned to me with a rubber-stamped DECLINED on the bottom. I'd been taking a lot of unauthorized days off in recent times and was now on an official final warning: if I ever took time off again without permission, I would be sacked. Hence the importance of persuading my boss that I really, really needed to go. I felt that he might make an exception if I begged.

My boss was known as the Commander. Not some megalomaniacal title he'd bestowed upon himself, but his navy rank during the war. This impressed me deeply, as it put him on the same level as James Bond. The Commander was a rugby man, and he still played, despite being in his sixties. I'd always got on well with him, although I had a feeling that he was finally losing patience with me, as evidenced by that warning.

His office was huge. As I sat across from him, separated by a vast desk cluttered with military memorabilia, I soon sensed that the meeting was not going to go my way.

'Out of the question, I'm afraid,' he said, with seemingly genuine regret. 'It's time for you to knuckle down and work hard. No more time off. You do know that if you do it again, you'll be dismissed?'

I nodded.

'You could do well here, David,' he continued, apparently seeing something in me that I hadn't seen in myself. 'Promotion to clerical officer isn't out of the question.'

I had no answer to that. The extra two pounds a week would be brilliant and I loved the idea of a more responsible position.

I felt invigorated and motivated, determined to climb the Civil Service ladder.

'I think your career is more important than a football match, don't you?' he added, showing me out of the door.

I murmured in agreement. He'd made a lot of sense. Apart from anything else, I wouldn't have been able to afford to go to the match without a job. There was a David Bowie concert in Eltham the following week, and that would cost me fifty pence, as well as the twenty pence bus fare. Plus, I was sure they'd show highlights from Upton Park on the news. I was OK with it. Really.

As it was lunchtime, I decided to forgo my usual egg and salad cream rolls (I wanted to save up my luncheon vouchers for a slap-up meal on Friday) and go for a walk along the Embankment. Instead of going past Temple tube station, I somehow found myself inside it, at the ticket office. My hastily formed plan was to reward myself for my self-discipline and commitment to a Civil Service career by going to West Ham's ground, buying a programme for my collection, then coming straight back to work. If I timed it right, I'd be gone a little over an hour.

I bought a ticket and heard the roar of an approaching train echoing in the tunnel as soon as I stepped on to the platform. It had UPMINSTER on the front, so it was the right one. There were plenty of seats in the last smoking carriage, with just a smattering of fans wearing claret and blue scarves on board. At every stop, more piled in. By the time we reached Aldgate East it was packed with football fans and the excitement and antici-pation were contagious.

It took me a while to work out why I was getting hostile looks from the West Ham fans: I was wearing my black and white Bromley scarf – the same colours as Hereford.

As we got off at Upton Park and stepped into Green Street,

I was astonished at the sight that greeted me. It was absolutely packed. It was as though half of London had taken the afternoon off work to be there. I pushed my way through to a programme seller, handed over ten pence for a couple of programmes and made my way back to the station, against the tide of people.

On the empty westbound platform, while waiting for the train back to work, I opened the programme and studied the teams. West Ham, on paper, were a terrifying prospect, especially from the perspective of a side occupying fourth place in the Southern League. Up front they had Geoff Hurst, who'd famously got a hat-trick against West Germany in the 1966 World Cup final, and Clyde Best, who'd somewhat less famously got a hat-trick against Bromley in a pre-season friendly. I imagined the Hereford players sitting in their changing room, nervously thinking about Hurst and Best as well as Brooking, 'Pop' Robson, Lampard, Bonds, Moore and Redknapp, and wishing they were back in Wales. Or wherever Hereford was.

Eventually my train appeared and the doors slid open. I got on and easily found a seat, from where I gazed enviously at the hundreds of fans making their way to the ground. And then, just as the train was about to leave, I found myself jumping up and making a mad dash for the doors. There was just enough of a gap for me to squeeze through and get back on the platform. As I stood and watched the train pull away without me, I realized that the Commander had only been almost right when he'd said that my career was more important than a football match. It actually depended on which football match. And this was one I couldn't miss, even if it cost me my job. It was the chance to witness giant-killing on an unprecedented scale. I was a bit concerned about being out of work, as unemployment had recently topped a million for the first time, but that was something I could worry about tomorrow.

Using the 'pen portraits' in the programme, I quickly familiarized myself with my team. The resolute Fred Potter, I learned, was a fence erector. I stifled a giggle after reading that. Dudley Tyler, Hereford's impressive inside-forward, had had an eight-hour hole-in-the-heart operation when he was a junior and was now an accounts clerk, learning computer work. Most interesting of all, to me anyway, was the story of captain Tony Gough, a right-winger turned right-back. He'd played in the Second Division for Swindon the previous season but wanted to work part time as an engineer so he dropped down to the Southern League. The rest of the team had occupations ranging from carpenter to foreman at a steel works. It was the classic non-league team.

Back on Green Street, the crowd seemed even thicker than before and it was a relief finally to reach the turnstile and hand over the seventy pence I'd been saving for the Bowie concert (West Ham didn't have special rates for the soon-to-be-unemployed). It was seating room only and I'd got there just in time: minutes later came an announcement that the ground was full, and there was still an hour before kick-off.

West Ham were determined to have a good FA Cup run. A fortnight earlier they'd been knocked out of the League Cup by Stoke in a dramatic semi-final. Bobby Moore had been forced to take over in goal and saved a penalty. The impact of this was slightly lessened when the Stoke player followed up to net the rebound.

There was a roar as a handful of Hereford players in suits (I had no idea who they were, although one of them looked particularly resolute) wandered on to the pitch and quickly walked off again at the sight of the biggest crowd any of them had ever played in front of.

The game itself was notable for its lack of surprises,

although the atmosphere made it one of the most enjoyable matches I'd been to. Like West Germany before them, Hereford United were on the receiving end of a Geoff Hurst hat-trick, which put the home side out of reach by half time.

Billy Meadows scored a well-deserved consolation goal late in the second half, although a bigger consolation for Hereford may have been the £40,000 they earned from their magnificent run. (Meadows had an incredibly tenuous link to West Ham: when he was a junior, he'd had a couple of seasons with Arsenal, when Hammers manager Ron Greenwood was a coach at Highbury.) His header made the scoreline a respectable 3–1, and I'd swear that every single one of the 42,271 fans stood and gave Hereford a standing ovation that lasted long after the last player had left the field.

After that it was back to reality for everyone involved. Next up for West Ham was a visit from Crystal Palace for a First Division clash; Hereford would be making the journey to Nuneaton for a Southern League cup tie; and I would be off to the Employment Exchange to look for a new job.

I was determined to find work straight away. You didn't make enough on the dole to buy records and watch football. Sure enough, by the time my P45 from Somerset House had arrived in the post, I had a new job. My breaking away from the Civil Service hadn't been entirely successful, however, as I would now be working as a statistician at the Commonwealth Secretariat, another government agency. I'd left the interview convinced that I wouldn't be getting the job because, although everything had gone well, there was the small matter of a reference. I later learned that the Commander had given me a glowing recommendation. We met up once a week for lunch after that and became good friends.

I couldn't wait to start my new career and just hoped there would be no more big games played on weekday afternoons.

And as luck would have it, the strike ended and midweek games went back to being played under lights in the evenings.

Life was good. I'd got lucky and found a job I really wanted. And things were about to get even better. At a party a few months later I met a girl called Mandy.

MANCHESTER UNITED

FOOTBALL LEAGUE DIVISION ONE
SATURDAY 16 DECEMBER 1972

OFFICIAL CLUB PROGRAMME INCLUDING 'LEAGUE FOOTBALL' PRICE 7p

10

Crystal Palace v. Manchester United, 16 December 1972

Manchester United! What magic that name holds for young and old alike. A visit from United – whether they be top or bottom of the league – is a virtual guarantee of a capacity attendance.

From the official programme

Mandy was my first proper, official girlfriend. We were both seventeen and she was everything I'd ever dreamed of – pretty, blonde and bubbly with the added bonus of living a few minutes' walk from a First Division football ground. We'd been officially going out for four months when, with Christmas approaching, she had asked if she could come along the next time I went to a game, as she'd never been to one. The fixture list gods must have been smiling on me because the following weekend the mighty Manchester United were playing just down the road from her, at Crystal Palace.

Mandy was still at school, so her parents only allowed me to come over once during the week, on Wednesday nights to watch *Van Der Valk*, a TV series about a maverick Dutch detective. On Thursday nights, she came to my place to watch *Top of the Pops*. Apart from watching TV and going to see Tutankhamun at the British Museum, we hadn't really done much together apart from sit on the swings in the park for hours on end, sit in the Wimpy bar for hours on end and hang around the bus shelter for hours on end, so the chance to watch football together was a welcome breakthrough.

I immediately drifted off into a fantasy that had me spending much more time with Mandy. She would get so captivated by the brilliance of Denis Law and his teammates that she would fall in love with Manchester United. So much so that when I passed my scooter driving test she'd want to go all over the country with me, watching them play and staying overnight in places like Norwich, Manchester and Leicester. I'd even be able to get cut-price accommodation as the Civil Service Union had 'negotiated a 5% discount on selected hotels for all our members'.

United weren't having a great season, but it was going a lot better than Palace's, who were already looking like going down. They'd only won twice in twenty-one games and were firmly rooted at the bottom of the table. My strategy was to impress Mandy with my football knowledge, believing this would somehow make her fancy me more.

After I'd parked my scooter in her dad's coal shed, we walked to the ground. With my arm around her, I filled her in on the game we were about to watch. 'Man U should win it easy,' I said, with the authority of someone who knew his football, 'two or three nil. Denis Law to get on the scoresheet.'

'Man U?'

'Yeah, that's what we call Manchester United. Crystal Palace are Palace.'

She seemed satisfied with this explanation of what authentic football supporters called the teams.

We went through the turnstiles at the Holmesdale Road End and on to the terraces, where it was so cold that I briefly considered getting us a hot Bovril, which I hated. It was my ambition to find a football ground that didn't sell Bovril, but I'd had no luck so far. Some grounds even sold Bovril-flavoured crisps as well.

There was a massive crowd, and the ground seemed absolutely packed. We were in with the Palace fans, which was down to a slight miscalculation on my part. Still, Mandy seemed happy, and she looked great. She was wearing my favourite outfit of hers – pink suedette jacket with big woolly sleeves, tight jeans and platform boots. When she started rubbing her hands together to keep warm, I offered her my gloves, which she accepted.

Flicking through the programme with frozen fingers, my heart sank. I learned that the wayward genius George Best wouldn't be playing, despite rumours earlier in the week that he was back in training. He had been more wayward than genius over the past few months and had been dropped for his frequent unexplained absences – something I had so far got away with in my Civil Service statistician's job. Bobby Charlton was also out, while the great Denis Law was only substitute. My favourite Football League team was falling apart, but I had every faith in the new breed, like Tony Young, Tommy O'Neill and Wyn Davies, becoming household names. Mandy seemed keen to know more about these players and I was touched by her interest, especially since I'd failed to share her David Cassidy obsession (I'd claimed to be a huge fan of his when we first met, but had only said this so she'd go out with me).

She didn't seem quite so impressed with the music coming over the loudspeakers. It was the new Crystal Palace club song (available for 50p from the Social Section shop), which went: 'We are the boys who wear claret and blue, and what we're doing we're doing for you, all our supporters are second to none, three cheers for Palace of Division One.'

Thankfully, it soon ended and the teams came out. Palace were playing in their new shirts, based on the Ajax Amsterdam strip but with purple and claret stripes instead of red. The theory was that it would help them play like Ajax, but it didn't. They had just been playing like Crystal Palace. This new strip had created a storm of controversy in the Subbuteo community due to the poor paintwork on the tiny figures, which had led to the colours overrunning each other. I thought it would be best not to draw attention to the fact that I still played Subbuteo at the age of seventeen so I didn't mention this to Mandy and found something else to talk about.

'See that bloke there?' I said, pointing to a man in an ill-fitting tracksuit climbing into one of the dugouts. 'That's Frank O'Farrell, the Man U gaffer.'

I liked saying the word 'gaffer'. I felt it made me the same as proper footballers, who always referred to 'the gaffer' in interviews. I thought I saw a new respect for my command of football lingo in Mandy's eyes, but wasn't sure. It could have been confusion. Perhaps it was a mistake trying to get her excited over the charisma-free United gaffer.

I decided to let United's football do the talking, and their first attack, ending with a powerful shot from Ian Moore that John Jackson did well to save, made me feel a lot more relaxed. A few minutes later, the same player came even closer to scoring. I kept glancing over at Mandy to see if she was enjoying herself and she seemed captivated by the on-field action. I felt a warm glow of satisfaction at this coming together of my two loves.

But then, after twenty-odd minutes, I had the first inkling of my plan backfiring in spectacular manner. A brilliant pass by Palace's Don Rogers put Paddy Mulligan in space and he coolly sidefooted past Alex Stepney.

'That was just *great*!' screamed Mandy, caught up in the crowd's excitement. 'Who was that?' she added breathlessly.

'Paddy Mulligan, the skipper,' I said with forced enthusiasm, even though my heart was sinking. 'Took his chance well,' I added knowledgeably. 'Nice pass from Rogers.'

The next goal showed that United hadn't learned their lesson: Rogers once again put Mulligan in to make it 2–0. This time Mandy didn't need to ask who scored the goal. Or who created it.

Reality was dawning. The team that had won the European Cup was gone. In its place was a distinctly second-rate version, with a gaffer to match. My mind began to drift and I found myself using my statistician skills to work out that the massive-sideburns-to-Crystal-Palace-player ratio was 1:1.67, which I scribbled into my programme, along with other match statistics such as the official attendance of 42,711. Mandy didn't seem to hear me when I told her the news. She was too wrapped up in the game, for all the wrong reasons. Palace had picked today of all days to start playing like Ajax, and Mandy was falling in love with them right in front of my eyes.

Then came the moment that was destined to be repeated in school playgrounds up and down the country for many months to come. Don Rogers found himself in plenty of space, beat what was left of the dispirited United defence, put the ball one side of Stepney, ran around the other side, and tapped the ball into the unguarded net. The only consolation was that I'd witnessed what was sure to be *Match of the Day*'s Goal of the Season. It was the kind of thing George Best used to do before he lost interest in being George Best.

I felt about as shellshocked as Man U's ashen-faced gaffer looked. Mandy was jumping and clapping along with the entire Holmesdale Road End. I remember thinking that it couldn't get any worse.

And then it did.

Alan Whittle, Palace's new signing from Everton, with blond curly hair and non-matching brown sideburns, exchanged passes with Hughes on the edge of the area before curling the ball past Stepney for what would surely be the runner-up in Goal of the Season. It was 4–0. My world was collapsing around me.

Don Rogers completed my afternoon of misery. He bore down on the United goal, his slug-like moustache glistening in the floodlights. Alex Stepney just stood there, seemingly rooted to the spot, before obligingly falling over, leaving Hughes the simple task of tapping in Palace's fifth goal, which was greeted by screams of 'GOAL!' from the Palace faithful and my girlfriend.

But there was to be one final twist of the knife. As the referee, John Hunting of Leicester, blew for full time, a familiar tune started playing over the loudspeakers: 'So let us hear your voices roar, for when we do we are sure to score. We'll do our best and with luck we'll win through, and all your cheering will see our dream come true. Let's hear your voices and give it the gun, so three cheers for Palace, hip hip hooray . . .' The Palace fans sensibly ignored their new song and began singing 'easy, easy' instead.

And it really had been. They'd got five but it could easily have been ten. Mandy was glowing with excitement. She was well and truly hooked. It was just on the wrong team. On the way back to her house she could talk of nothing but the genius of Don Rogers, the cool head of Paddy Mulligan and the athleticism of John Jackson. I should have known that my plan was overly ambitious. If you have a team of world beaters at the end of your road, you probably won't look elsewhere for a team to support.

Still, the true benefit of going out with someone who lived so close to a ground became apparent only after the game, when we got back to her place in time to watch the Teleprinter on *Grandstand* – something I usually had to watch in a shop window. We also sat through a match report of the game we'd just seen, which made Man U sound even worse than they were.

As I wheeled my scooter out of the coal shed and made my way out of SE25, I realized that we wouldn't be heading up to Old Trafford on Saturday afternoons. There'd be no nights of passion in hotels throughout the north-west. Instead, Mandy and I would be making the short walk to Selhurst Park every other week.

And that was how it worked out. In a stunning piece of role reversal, we watched Mandy's favourite team a lot that season, even though they were generally terrible and were relegated at the end of it. I was happy just to be with her, and even developed quite a soft spot for her team, especially Don Rogers, who was playing like George Best, even though he looked more like a bus conductor. At least we didn't have to go to any away games – Mandy simply wasn't interested. And I even managed to persuade her to watch a few Bromley games when Palace weren't playing at home.

Recently, I looked Mandy up on Facebook to see what she was up to these days. Instead of a profile photo, she had the Crystal Palace club badge.

When football gets you, it gets you for life.

QUEENS PARK RANGERS

WARWICK WRIGHT

Season 1975-76	LEAGUE DIVISION ONE
ARSENAL	
Monday 19th April 1976	ko 11 a.m.
OFFICIAL COLOUR SOUVENIR PROGRAMME	**15 p**

11

Queens Park Rangers v. Arsenal,
19 April 1976

I gave a lot of the lads a pile of tomatoes last summer and I get
tremendous satisfaction from the quiet life.

Dave Thomas, from the official programme

Leaving home had been so easy, I'd done it four times. On each
occasion, with my parents thinking that they'd finally got rid of
me, I turned up on their doorstep a few weeks later with
my possessions (including programmes) in half a dozen
Sainsbury's bags, mumbling something about how I'd just been
unfairly sacked from my latest job and hadn't been able to
afford my rent. My bed was always made and my room ready.
It was almost as though they knew I'd be back.

But then, at my twenty-first birthday party, which was
held at a local scout hall, I was talking to a girl and she asked
where I lived. Suddenly, 'with my mum and dad' didn't seem
the kind of answer that would lead to the hoped-for birthday
snog to 10cc's 'I'm Not in Love' and I realized I had to
move out, for good. My mum would be pleased. She had
taken to leaving the 'To Let' page of the *Bromley Advertiser*

lying around, with suggestions helpfully circled in red ink.

One of these was a small bedsit in Beckenham, which I wanted to move into as soon as I saw it. My dad paid three months' rent in advance, rented me a black and white TV, and gave me a lift to various job interviews. I eventually succeeded in becoming a security guard for 20th Century Electronics, a factory in Croydon. I was surprised by the ease with which I got the position, although a little less surprised when I learned that the factory produced parts for nuclear reactors. Perhaps there weren't a lot of other candidates.

With a new home and new job also came a new social life. I started hanging out at the Three Tuns in Beckenham with a bunch of art student types, with whom I had everything in common apart from one crucial thing: none of them liked football. Or so I thought until one young man called Mick, whose hair was clearly modelled on Rick Wakeman's, came into the pub one night wearing a QPR scarf. It turned out he was a life-long fan of theirs, which until now had been an unrewarding existence given their history of consistent underachievement. But under Dave Sexton they had not only become one of the most exciting sides of the era, they were also having the most successful season in their history. I had always been willing to jump on the nearest bandwagon, so when Mick invited me along to the Easter Monday fixture against Arsenal, I readily agreed, especially as I needed some respite from a miserable run of Bromley defeats, the latest of them an eight-goal thrashing at the hands of Chesham.

He picked me up in his black Ford Zephyr and we set off for Shepherd's Bush, excitedly discussing what lay ahead. As I finished my breakfast of a Crunchie Easter egg, Mick reminded me that the Hoops, as he called them, were neck and neck with Liverpool in the title race and a win today would put them top, if only for a few hours. Although I always liked watching them on TV, I wasn't quite ready to adopt QPR as my favourite big team, following earlier flirtations with Manchester United (The Lawman), Fulham (my first game), Arsenal (trying to impress skinheads) and Crystal Palace (Mandy). I'd decided to see how my first experience of watching them live went.

When we got within the stadium's shadow, we parked in one of the nearby streets and walked the few hundred yards to the ground. The police presence around Loftus Road was reassuringly massive. They were clearly taking no chances, right down to getting the kick-off brought forward to prevent rival fans drinking before the match. I was pleased with this as I was feeling unusually anxious. There had been plenty of rumours about the Arsenal fans trying to take over the Loft End, where Mick normally stood, and although I was a security guard, I was far from a fearless one. A few nights earlier I was on duty when I thought I heard footsteps echoing through the empty factory. I never did find out who or what it was as I was hiding under my desk.

We went into the ground, and after nervously glancing around for red and white scarves we got down to the serious business of reading the programme, starting with the team line-ups. Arsenal were mainly notable for having the First Division's best passer in Liam Brady, and the First Division's baldest defender in Terry Mancini, while the QPR team was full of great players. They were so good that they had been dubbed 'The Team of All Talents' (admittedly by their own programme editor). One of the best players I'd ever seen, Don Rogers, formerly of Crystal Palace, was only in the reserves.

Of those who would be starting today, one name stood out for me: the QPR number 7. The last time I'd seen Dave Thomas he was known as David Thomas (Bishop Auckland) and we were both schoolboys. He was on the wing that day at Wembley when England beat Germany and had scored the winning goal. His habit of wearing his socks rolled down was already established in that game and I inevitably copied it as soon as I went back to school. The programme gave me a glimpse into his life away from football, as he revealed that he was now fifty-fourth in line for a vegetable allotment from Wokingham Council. As a role model, I could only respect him for being in touch with everyday life, but on balance I think I preferred George Best and his shagging of four Miss Worlds.

When Mick and I first bonded over football, he'd shown me his collection of programmes and it was clear that QPR's was the best I'd ever seen. It had a checkerboard design on the cover which changed colours every game – today's was red and white – and was full of the sort of detailed information I craved, from weather reports from recent games (St James's Park was bright but windy the previous Saturday) to the fact that I was about to witness QPR's 2,973rd professional match. No wonder it had just picked up the programme world's highest honour, the Charles Tew Trophy. I'd been desperately hoping it would win ever since finding out it was on the shortlist. Ron Philips, the editor, fully deserved it.

The players ran out, QPR looking particularly good in their snazzy tracksuits. The game started at a sluggish pace, as though all twenty-two players had, like me, overdone the Easter eggs. Arsenal's tactic of playing ten men in defence made for a dull first half, and QPR squandered chance after chance. It seemed that the pressure of winning a must-win game had got to them and their confidence was visibly draining away. Even Dave Thomas, whose runs down the wing at Wembley had thrilled me so much, was out of sorts. The only real entertainment came from the running battle between a petulant Stan Bowles and anyone wearing an Arsenal shirt.

It was almost a relief when Mr Nippard's whistle signalled the end of the first half and I could get on with reading the programme. I'd recently started saving the last six pages to read at half time and now I eagerly turned to page fifteen, which was the 'Ranger to Ranger' page.

I was so deeply engrossed in a rather confusing letter from a Russian fan by the name of Slavo Cimeron which read 'Dear footbal club, O skal be uery glach if I get of you the photograph ad the badge of your club' that I almost missed the announcement that would change my life. I was vaguely aware that a string of numbers was being read out over the Tannoy and when I thought I heard '3827' it rang the slightest of bells in the back of my mind.

'What did he just say?' I asked Mick, who was busy devouring one of Loftus Road's famous meat pies.

'Dunno – just the lucky draw winners, I think,' he said, spraying me with crumbs.

'Did he say three eight two seven?'

Mick shrugged his shoulders and got back to his meat pie. I was grateful that he'd opted for non-verbal communication. Besides, I was sure that I'd heard '3827'.

The good thing about having an uncommon interest in programmes is that you know exactly where everything is, even after quickly glancing through it once. I immediately turned to page four and there it was: LUCKY NO. DRAW – Number 3827. The prize was better than mere money, it was one of the tracksuit tops worn by the QPR players as they came out on to the field. They were made by Gola. I knew this because they had GOLA in huge letters plastered across the front. And I was pretty sure I'd won one. If only they could repeat the winning numbers.

As if in response to my silent plea, the announcer started running through the winning numbers again, and sure enough, 3827 was among them. 'To pick up your top,' he announced in an overexcited Radio One DJ kind of way, 'bring your programme to the South Africa Road entrance after the match.'

The second half seemed to last for ever. All I wanted was to hear the final whistle so I could collect my prize. I kept glancing at Mick Leach, the QPR substitute, who sat on the bench wearing his tracksuit top. I thought he looked great in it and imagined how I would look when I finally put mine on.

At least the on-field action was an improvement on the first half. Brian Kidd, who wasn't even listed to play, gave Arsenal a shock lead ten minutes after the break to put QPR's record of never having lost a home game on 19 April (another interesting statistic from the programme) at risk. His weak shot somehow went under Phil Parkes in a bizarre echo of a similar incident involving the same two players at Highbury the previous Christmas. Within two minutes, the scores were level: Frank McLintock MBE got on the scoresheet against his old club by converting Don Masson's free kick, to send the Loft End into ecstasy.

Then, just as time was starting to run out for QPR, Stan Bowles went on a run and beat a couple of defenders in the box before being caught in an ungainly tackle by Richie Powling. He went down with a flamboyant dive that was enough to convince Mr Nippard of Christchurch to point to the spot. Despite angry and possibly justified protests from the Arsenal players, Gerry Francis stayed calm and slotted the penalty just inside the post for the winner.

QPR were top of the league, and I was about to own a tracksuit top worn by one of their players. I just hoped it wasn't Dave Thomas's. Although I hero-worshipped him to an embarrassing degree, I was realistic enough to realize that while he was smallish and slim, I was not. The man handing out the prizes was easy to find as he was standing by the gate with a small pile of blue tops. After I showed him the number in my programme, he took one look at my physique and picked out a top with 'Size 42-44 Chest' on the label.

'Whose is it?' I asked excitedly, having narrowed it down to a shortlist of David Webb, Frank McLintock and Gerry Francis.

'Yours, mate,' he answered dryly, before turning his attention to a slight elderly woman who was also, it appeared, among the winners. She would find it much easier to fit into one of the smaller sizes.

I didn't pursue the matter of previous ownership as I was far too thrilled to be holding the magnificent top, which was dark blue with white cuffs and zipped halfway up the front.

Unlike the previous Easter Monday when it had snowed, it was a warm day, but I still couldn't resist slipping it on over my tank top. It was a perfect fit, and I was delighted to get a few envious looks from passing Rangers fans. This wasn't the first time I'd acquired clothing belonging to someone famous. A couple of years earlier, on a Capital Radio phone-in, I had managed to drunkenly persuade Woody of the Bay City Rollers to send me a pair of his blue, black and white socks in return for a donation to some charity. He was as good as his word, and it was only when I got the socks that I realized I didn't have a clue what to do with them. If only eBay had been around in 1974.

But this top was something I'd be able to wear all the time. And that's exactly what I did. I wore it every time I went out, to parties, to work, sometimes even to bed. I wore it to kick-abouts down at the park, imagining that it would somehow turn me from a mediocre footballer into a great one, in the same way that Billy's Boots in the *Tiger* comic transformed him into one of the best players of his generation.

The top quickly became an important part of my life. I never tired of telling people where it came from and had even embellished the details slightly, to give the impression that David Webb had handed it to me personally.

One day, The Grubby and I were playing 'three and in' down

at Bromley Park. It was mid July and the temperature was in the high twenties. As it was summer, the goalposts had been taken down and we were using his green cord jacket as one post and my QPR top as the other. After a while we decided it was too hot to carry on playing and adjourned to the Shortlands Tavern for a couple of lager and limes.

It was only after we'd been sitting inside drinking for about half an hour that I realized we'd left our tops behind. I dashed back to the park, chest heaving with anxiety, and saw that The Grubby's coat lay exactly where he'd left it. But my QPR top was gone.

In a blind panic, I searched everywhere for it, thinking that it might have somehow blown into the bushes, despite a complete absence of wind, but eventually I had to admit that it had gone for ever. I sat down, devastated, wondering why anyone else would want a tatty old tracksuit top.

Whether or not this played a part in my decision to move away from the area, I don't know. Dave, my best friend, had moved to Wantage, a market town near Oxford, and was insisting I join him there. I worked out my week's notice at 20th Century Electronics, packed my important possessions into several Sainsbury's bags and took the coach to Oxford Bus Station, where Dave picked me up in his lime-green Mini and took me to my new home.

SAINTS

Southampton Football Club

FOOTBALL LEAGUE DIVISION II
SATURDAY OCTOBER 2nd 1976
KICK-OFF 3.00 pm.
TODAY'S VISITORS

FULHAM

OFFICIAL PROGRAMME 15p

12

Southampton v. Fulham,
2 October 1976

Until Fulham struck upon the idea of entering the field of nostalgia by signing Rodney Marsh and George Best, they had to rub along on gates of nine thousand. Now they top the 25,000 mark.

From the official programme

Decisions made after eight pints and four cans of lager are rarely good ones

Dave and I were in the Swan in Wantage, getting overly emotional about the genius of George Best, when Terry, a dour, friendless, trenchcoat-encased hippy, plopped himself down at our table, uninvited. He sat staring silently at his half-pint glass as we continued to swap memories of the greatest player we had ever seen, and I felt confident that he would soon be driven away, his usual solitary reflection preferable to moist-eyed football worship.

As far as we knew, Terry wasn't passionate about anything. He was a student, and since we avoided him at parties, we knew little about him other than that. He rarely even spoke. True to form, he just sat there listening to our alcohol-fuelled ramblings. It was surely only a matter of time before boredom sent him away.

And then, just after I'd finished reliving George's brilliant tackle on his own teammate, Rodney Marsh, in the Fulham v. Hereford game which we'd seen on TV the previous weekend, Terry came to life for, as far as we were aware, the first time. 'United against Spurs, seventy-one,' he announced in a trembling voice, and we gasped, as much in surprise at this unexpected interruption as in anticipation of what was coming next. 'George gets the ball just outside the six-yard box,' he continued. 'Everyone's expecting him to blast it. Instead, he glances up and casually lobs the ball over *four* defenders *plus* the keeper. And get this' – he was almost choking with emotion now – 'he doesn't even celebrate. He just smiles and casually raises his arm, as though this was the kind of thing he did every day.'

Dave and I sat there, our mouths open. Terry had revealed himself to be something we never could have expected. Hippies didn't like football, everyone knew that. But after this initial outburst, there was no stopping him. Terry's stature in our eyes grew even more when he told us that he'd once written a ten-page letter to George, and we became inseparable friends when he pulled a well-worn copy of *Best: An Intimate Biography* by Michael Parkinson from his rucksack. By closing time, we knew the evening couldn't just finish there, so we loaded up on Carlsberg cans and returned to the house Dave and I shared with an engineer called Robbie.

At around five in the morning, after drinking possibly the twentieth toast to George since we'd arrived, Terry said, 'Anyone know where Fulham are playing today?'

There was silence as the implications of his question sank in. In typically contrary fashion, George had recently signed for the Second Division club (which was a step up from his previous English league team, Stockport County). Because he was George Best, he had scored seventy-one seconds into his debut and there had been rumblings in the press that he was starting to look like the George Best of old, a theory boosted by a flurry of goals and an outstanding performance against Hereford.

'I'm pretty sure it's Southampton away,' I said. 'They're bottom of the table.'

'We must go there, *we must see George*!' shouted Terry, with newly revealed passion.

He was right. We decided that it was too late to get any sleep, so we'd have some breakfast then hitch to the ground, which was around sixty miles from Wantage. Going to the game would mean missing *TISWAS*, our Saturday morning TV ritual, but we wouldn't be able to do both. Before we left we used an old cardboard box to make a sign with SOUTHAMPTON on it, which Terry folded and placed carefully in his rucksack, and then persuaded our flatmate Robbie, who was already up and exercising, to give us a lift to the A34 at great personal cost – he wouldn't need to do any tidying, cleaning or cooking for a fortnight. In a move I felt showed a complete lack of trust, he made us sign a note to this effect.

After I'd fed my cat Pigdog (whose name was a legacy of my *Valiant*-reading, German-footballer-taunting youth), we got into Robbie's Ford Capri and fifteen minutes later were dropped off at my favourite hitching spot, just outside Harwell. It was always a good place to get an early morning lift as there were plenty of commuters heading to London and Oxford. What hadn't registered was that since this was a Saturday, most commuters wouldn't be commuting.

Although it was after seven o'clock, it was still dark. We took it in turns to hold the SOUTHAMPTON sign and stick out a thumb, while the other two sat on the grass verge, shivering under an orange street light. As daylight arrived and the effects of alcohol started to wear off, the stupidity of what we were doing began to pierce my consciousness. Just as I was about to suggest abandoning our mission, a horse transporter pulled up twenty yards past us. We ran towards it and asked the driver, a middle-aged man wearing a cloth cap, where he was heading.

'Bath racecourse,' he said. 'Any good?'

Dave and I looked at each other, unsure if Bath was on the way to Southampton or not. Luckily, Terry evidently had a better sense of geography than we did and took the initiative. 'Yeah, that would be great, thanks,' he said.

The driver looked at us, as though weighing up whether this was really a good idea, before saying, 'OK, jump in then.'

This was brilliant. We had five and a half hours to get to the ground, which should leave us plenty of time to get lunch in Southampton. We climbed in and thanked him profusely.

The smell of horses wasn't a problem as Dave and I managed to drown it out completely with the smell of Brut, as worn by Liverpool's Kevin Keegan. We were still at the age of thinking that pulling power was in direct proportion to the amount of aftershave we splashed on, so, in an increasingly desperate battle to be the most attractive of the two Daves, each of us now got through a bottle every ten days or so. The driver, whose name was Henry, was kind enough not to say anything.

Thanks to *Shoot* magazine, I knew that Mick Channon, who would be playing for Southampton, was a big fan of racing. This would be an excellent conversation starter with Henry, and would break the awkward silence that had settled over the cabin.

'So, what do you think of Mick Channon?' I asked him.

'Who's he?'

'He's a footballer who likes horseracing.'

'I see,' replied Henry, before silence once again descended over us.

'Do you have a map, please?' I asked twenty minutes later.

'There's one in the glovebox.'

I'd heard that people usually picked up hitchhikers for company, in which case Henry must have been severely disappointed. Perhaps tiring of my attempts at conversation, he put his radio on and we listened to Radio One's new DJ, Kid Jensen.

Against a backdrop of 'Combine Harvester' by The Wurzels, I spread the map out on my lap and soon discovered that we were heading in pretty much the opposite direction to where we needed to go. The good news was that if we could somehow find the M3, we'd be back on track.

And that was when fate intervened. At a roundabout, I spotted a sign saying M3, BOURNEMOUTH/SOUTHAMPTON/PORTSMOUTH.

'Can you drop us off here, please?' I asked excitedly, and a relieved-looking Henry deposited us by the side of the road. As he took off again, I noticed he'd opened all his windows wide, to give the cabin a good airing.

From our point of view, the hard part was done. It was now a straight road to Southampton and we had the best part of five hours to get there. Terry got the neatly folded sign out of his rucksack and selflessly took first shift at holding it, thumb outstretched. Rain started to fall, but our spirits were high.

We waited. And waited. And waited. There were soon only three hours until kick-off. Then two. Then one. We were now in serious danger of missing the game and started bickering among ourselves, blaming one another for the lack of cars stopping. Terry even had the bright idea of adding PLEASE to his sign, but it didn't seem to make any difference. Apparently no one wanted to pick up three soaked, sulky, scruffy young lads.

We grew increasingly demoralized. The thought of missing a hatful of classic George goals was almost unbearable. We seemed destined to spend the next chunk of our lives on an obscure motorway ramp miles from home, while the great man weaved his magic on the bottom-of-the-table Southampton defence at The Dell.

Then suddenly, midway through the first half and after several hours of watching cars whizz past us, a Terry lookalike in a beaten-up VW slowed down and came to a halt. Seeing the red brakelights got my heart beating rapidly with excitement. Kevin, the driver, just nodded at us knowingly, and uttered the word 'karma'. We got in and Terry sat in the front, taking care of the conversation, while Dave and I took the back seat where we sat in a cloud of Brut. The driver didn't know where the ground was, which I saw as conclusive proof that *most* hippies don't like football, but said he'd drop us off in the city centre.

He was as good as his word, and half an hour later we were in the middle of Southampton, frantically looking around. Dave asked a woman where the football ground was and she gave us detailed directions. It was within walking distance, but we ran. It was now 3.55 by my watch so we were still in with a chance of watching the last half hour or so, as long as we could get there quickly. Eventually the floodlights came into view, and not long after that I saw a road sign saying THE DELL and heard the sound of the crowd. We arrived at the turnstiles dripping with sweat, but we'd made it. In a rare piece of good luck we didn't have to pay to get in, having missed about three quarters of the game.

Exhausted from all the physical exertion, we wearily clambered up the steep terracing just as a chorus of boos was ringing out. What was going on? We arrived at the top just in time to see a lone figure in a white shirt trudging off the pitch, head bowed. The referee, Lester Shapter (Paignton), was brandishing a red card and pointing towards the tunnel. I didn't need to see the number 7 on his back to know that the dismissed player was George Best.

According to the jubilant Saints fans standing next to us, George had taken exception to the awarding of a free kick and had made his displeasure known to Mr Shapter with an extensive rant. The only consolation was the possibility of George being the first player ever to get a red card (the card system was in operation for the first time that day), but he was narrowly beaten to that honour by Dave Wagstaffe of Blackburn.

We had hitched all the way to Southampton to see our hero walk sulkily off the pitch. We had major hangovers, we hadn't slept, and we would now have to stand in the rain and watch an irrelevant Second Division game that, without its main attraction, none of us would have watched even if it had been played in our back garden.

George's absence didn't just affect us. His teammates also seemed to lose interest, and Southampton looked anything but a bottom-of-the-table team. Their centuries-old left-winger Hugh Fisher (according to the previous week's Charlton programme, he'd made his debut in 1673) was tearing Fulham's defence to pieces, Mel Blyth (two) and Ted McDougall (two) adding the finishing touches. Even though we were only there for twenty minutes, we saw four goals and witnessed a George-less Fulham go down 4–1.

We couldn't face hitching back so we took the train from Southampton to Oxford, got the bus to Wantage, and arrived home tired, cold, hungry and broke.

Over the following days, once I'd got over the disappointment of our wasted trip to the south coast, I began to see events in a new light. It was because George Best did things differently that I was, with plenty of others, such a huge fan. So the fact he'd been sent off just after everyone had started to talk of his redemption and rebirth somehow made him more un-predictable and therefore even more admirable.

After he fell out with Fulham in 1977, I remained a fan during his subsequent spells at Los Angeles Aztecs, Fort Lauderdale Strikers, Detroit Express, Hibernian, San Jose Earthquakes, Sea Bees, Rangers of Hong Kong, Bournemouth, Newry Town and, finally, Brisbane Lions. The last time Dave and I saw him play was in a charity match in Swindon, where, at the age of thirty-six, he scored five goals to help his team to a 12–9 victory. But although that was something I'll never for-get, it wasn't my most memorable visit to Swindon's County Ground.

That came just seven weeks after the ill-fated journey to Southampton.

F.A. CUP First Round

Swindon Town

v

Bromley

Official Programme

10p

13

Swindon Town v. Bromley,
20 November 1976

Bromley has a splendid stadium at Hayes Lane with excellent
amenities, and floodlighting, and a fine drainage system which
is responsible for what is described as a perfect pitch.

From the official programme

I was on the production line, attaching a door to an MGB,
when I heard the news. One of the sales reps, a Swindon fan
known as Tony, due to his resemblance to the character who said
'great' all the time in *The Rise and Fall of Reginald Perrin*, rushed
up to me in a state of almost manic excitement.

'Guess who Swindon have drawn in the Cup?' he asked, even
though it was clear that he could barely wait to tell me.

'Oxford United?' I guessed, thinking that only being drawn
against their greatest rivals would cause such a state of
heightened arousal.

'No,' he said, slapping me on the back a little too hard, 'we're
at home to *Bromley*. Isn't it great?'

I had to lay down my pneumatic screwdriver and sit down to let
this sink in. That was the beauty of working for British Leyland:

there was plenty of time to sit around and let things sink in. There was also plenty of time to play football, smoke, play cards and sleep. Our factory was often cited by the Conservative opposition as all that was wrong with state-owned industries, and they had a point. The Transport and General Workers Union was so strong, we only had to make three cars every hour.

Tony announced that he'd be going to the ground (it was only a fifteen-minute drive) as soon as tickets went on sale, so he could make sure of getting the best seats. He then asked if I wanted him to get me a ticket. This sounded brilliant. Bromley's biggest game in my lifetime and I'd be getting a perfect view of the action.

The nearer it got to Saturday, the more nervous I became. My mum, resigned to the fact that I'd never grow out of my Bromley phase, had sent me the *Bromley and Kentish Times* preview and it seemed that local hopes were high. RARIN' TO GO – THAT'S BIDDLE'S BATTLERS screamed the back page, which went on to make the unlikely claim that manager John Biddle would walk home down the motorway if Bromley won. I hoped he wouldn't, as it would be an offence under subsection (4) of section 17 of the Road Traffic Regulation Act. I knew this because I'd recently been obsessively studying the Highway Code in preparation for my driving test.

As I didn't yet have my licence, I had to rely on public transport to get me to Swindon when the day of the match finally arrived. The bus took for ever to get there, stopping at just about every obscure village in Oxfordshire, including Letcombe Bassett, Childrey and Uffington. When I got to the ground, kick-off was only half an hour away.

I headed straight to the souvenir shop and was stunned at how much bigger it was than the one at Hayes Lane, which only sold pens, badges and old programmes. Swindon fans were spoiled. They could choose from nearly thirty products including teapot stands (55p), letter racks (60p) and bracelets (45p). This brought home to me the difference in scale between the two clubs.

After showing immense discipline and buying nothing more than a couple of programmes, I made my way up the steps in the two-tiered South Stand and eventually found my seat. Tony, who was already there with a bunch of salesman types, hadn't been exaggerating. It was high up in the stand, right on the halfway line, with a panoramic view of the ground. I'd never watched football from such a perfect position. Just behind us was the directors' box where, as the stadium announcer had pointed out, the Mayor of Swindon was the special guest. In the absence of any serious competition, he was probably the most famous person to watch Bromley since I'd been supporting them.

I lit up a Rothmans (I'd switched to them after they started sponsoring the Isthmian League) and, looking down at the un-covered terraces behind the goal to my left, saw Derek, Roy and Peter taking up their places. These were the people you would see at every Bromley game, home or away, the supporters who had an almost inexhaustible supply of optimism. They'd been good friends when I was growing up and the four of us had been to over a hundred games together. But then I'd moved away and we'd lost touch. It was a crisp winter day and I didn't envy them standing out in the open. As Derek looked around to take in the atmos-phere, I waved, but he didn't see me. Since the attendance was later given as 6,500, I shouldn't have been surprised.

When the teams ran out, it took a while to make the mental adjustment of seeing Bromley and a proper, successful league side on the same pitch. The contrast between our star players couldn't have been more stark. They had Trevor Anderson, the Northern Ireland international they'd signed from Manchester United, while we had John Duffy, described in the programme as 'one of the unfortunate band of unemployed at the moment', who was 'busy looking for work as a steeplejack'.

The programme was also of a much higher standard than

usual, although I had spotted a serious discrepancy, which I circled in the copy I used for notes. On page three it said, 'We have never played Bromley in any competition,' yet on the last page Doug Buswell, the Pools Manager (whatever that was), said, 'Welcome to Bromley. Having had many hard games against them in the past, I know full well they won't be a pushover.'

Mr Buswell was wrong about the hard games in the past as they were non-existent, unless they'd taken place on his Subbuteo pitch. I hoped that he was right about Bromley not being a pushover, though. There were plenty of positive signs. We'd lost only twice in the last twenty games and had put nine past Walton and Hersham in the previous round. The twin strikers, John Duffy and Junior Crooks, were on fire, with twenty-one goals between them in sixteen games. The *Bromley and Kentish Times* was so impressed, it had given them the nickname 'Smash and Grab'. And to complete the list, Swindon had lost their unbeaten home record the previous Saturday.

The signs may have been good, but I don't think I'd ever been as nervous at a football match in my life. Looking down at Derek and the rest of the Bromley boys, I began to suspect that my feeling of smugness for having such a good seat was misplaced. They were meant to be jealous of me, but I suddenly found myself envying them. I had a feeling of longing to be with them, wanting to share this adventure with the people I'd stood alongside as Bromley went through the worst of times.

I buttoned up my parka, wrapped my black and white scarf around my neck to keep out the cold, then got up. I couldn't believe what I was doing. Leaving the comfort of my perfect £1.75 seat so that I could stand in the freezing cold with an assortment of misfits behind the Swindon goal in the only uncovered part of the County Ground. I don't think Tony and his fellow salesmen even noticed I had gone. I went down the steps and pushed my way through the crowd, which was a first for me at a Bromley game, desperate to find my old friends.

I hadn't seen them for a couple of years, but immediately felt at home when I reached them. I was greeted with a warmth that made me wish I'd never left Bromley, with Roy, Derek and Peter in particular keen to find out what I'd been up to. After I'd filled in the gaps, talk inevitably turned to the vital game. This was the biggest Bromley fixture any of us had seen, and there was evidence of sleepless nights on several faces. Roy, who was always the biggest worrier, reckoned he hadn't even bothered going to bed because he knew that sleep would be impossible.

The game got underway, and Bromley were immediately under pressure. Swindon looked like taking a very early lead until Alan Hawkins cleared off the line with goalkeeper Malcolm Broadway beaten. It was obvious that the players were as nervous as we were and, not for the first time, I wondered why I put myself through this.

But then, after somehow surviving the first quarter of an hour, Bromley launched their first serious attack. David Mann drove a cross into the penalty area to where Phil Emblem was waiting, but the ball (donated by Eddie, Bob, Charlie and Win, according to the programme) got stuck in the mud before it could get to him. It all happened right in front of us. If only it had been hit just a little harder, we could have been a goal up.

Ten minutes later, the moment we had all been fearing arrived. Ray McHale volleyed home at the far post and it was 1–0 to Swindon. But Bromley didn't seem fazed. Gradually and inexplicably, they began to take control of the match. Junior Crooks, visibly growing in confidence, was the best player on the pitch, taking on the Swindon defenders in a series of thrilling runs, one of which led to a floating cross that was beautifully met by Derek Brown, who crashed the ball into the net in front of us. Before we had a chance to react, Mr Roost of Bath blew his whistle for offside.

Paul McCarthy was then put clean through a surprisingly hesitant defence. As goalkeeper Jim Allan raced out, everything seemed to happen in slow motion. The Bromley striker appeared to freeze in front of the baying Swindon crowd behind the goal and tamely shot at the grateful keeper. My heart was beating so fast that I was gulping for air.

Then, against the run of play, some pushing in the box resulted in a penalty to Swindon. Trevor Anderson lined up to take the kick against Malcolm Broadway. A Northern Ireland international against a driving instructor. I couldn't watch, but when the Irishman blasted his kick wide, we began to sense this was going to be our day. A feeling that grew when both Smash and Grab came close just after half time.

The home fans were getting anxious and were chanting for substitute Don Rogers to make an appearance. I was hoping he wouldn't. He'd already been responsible for crushing my dreams when he was at Crystal Palace and I didn't want him doing it a second time.

Perhaps getting a little ahead of ourselves, we began to feel that an equalizer wasn't beyond the bounds of possibility and started to talk about a potential replay at Hayes Lane, which we were sure would be all-ticket. Around this time, things took an unexpected and shocking turn.

When things go wrong, they can go wrong in different degrees: there's the slight blip, the character-testing reversal of fortune, and then there's the kind of mind-numbing catastrophe that almost causes the brain to shut down. The chain of events that unfolded just after the hour mark fell into the latter category and left the travelling fans wondering if they'd stumbled into a cruel nightmare. The sequence, according to the notes in my programme, went something like this:

63 minutes: Bromley concede goal to Syrett when Broadway fails to deal with cross.

64 minutes: Bromley concede goal to Moss with unstoppable shot.

70 minutes: Bromley concede goal to Anderson following goal-mouth scramble.

74 minutes: Bromley concede goal to Syrett again, as defence completely evaporates.

80 minutes: Bromley concede goal to Anderson again, with a far post header.

88 minutes: Bromley concede goal to Moss again, from a brilliant cross.

Bromley had simply run out of steam, after literally working themselves to a standstill. They'd given everything, and it was only Swindon's superior fitness that led to the inflated 7–0 score-line. In the bar afterwards, some of the players, like Junior Crooks, joined us and there was no shortage of Bromley – and Swindon – fans lining up to buy them drinks to show their appreciation.

I was dreading work on the Monday morning. I was already crushed and the last thing I needed was Tony coming over and gloating about the result. I forced a smile when I saw him make his way towards me and once again put down my pneumatic screwdriver, this time prepared for the insults.

'Your lot were great, weren't they?' he said with genuine admiration. 'You should be proud of them.'

And I was. It was probably the closest 7–0 game in history. If only the bounce of the ball had gone a little differently, John Biddle would still have been walking down the motorway when I clocked in that morning.

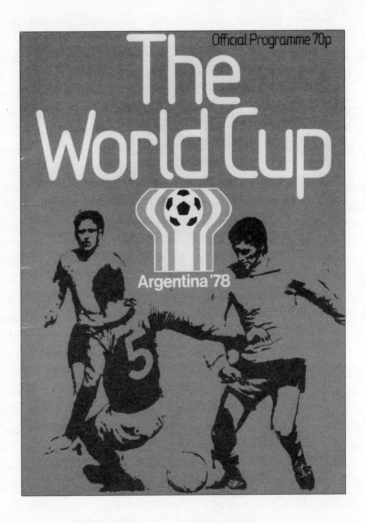

14

Argentina v. Peru,
21 June 1978

Buena suerte, Argentina!
From the official programme

I was on the coach, looking forward to the clash between Argentina and Peru, the most important game in the World Cup so far. Argentina, the hosts, were in serious trouble and needed a big win against a very good Peru side in order to make the next stage. I'd taken a few days off work at the MG factory in Abingdon as I'd been invited to watch the game on TV in Milton Keynes. Under normal circumstances, that is not an enticing prospect. But when you're twenty-three and you've been asked by the girl on whom you've had a major crush for two years, then it's enough to cause a sensory overload as you eagerly anticipate the heady cocktail of football and love.

Her name was Cathy, and the invitation had been given at her sister's eighteenth birthday party in Wantage, where I was living, the previous weekend. We'd been really good friends for ages. She was one of the first people I met when I moved there and we often went to concerts (The Adverts, Eddie and the Hot

Rods) and films (*Grease*, *Taxi Driver*) together. Despite this, I was always too scared to ask her out properly.

Then, a few months earlier, she'd moved to Milton Keynes to study. We talked on the phone a couple of times a week, but the party was the first time I'd seen her since she left Wantage. I'd always had a huge crush on her, so was ecstatic when our 'just good friends' status changed after we got through a Watney's Party Seven and a couple of bottles of Stingo Barley Wine ('strong as a double scotch, less than half the price') between us. Since neither of us was a great drinker, we found ourselves in a kind of relaxed haze and suddenly started kissing, which was what I'd dreamed about since first meeting her. We sat on a beanbag in the corner for the rest of the night, bodies entwined, snogging as though we'd just discovered it – which wouldn't have been too much of an exaggeration in my case.

Later, when we were talking, I'd told her how much I was looking forward to the Argentina v. Peru fixture, and that was when she invited me up to her flat to watch it. She also said that I could stay the night.

The game didn't kick off until 11.15 p.m., so Cathy had asked me to get there at nine for dinner, which she'd be cooking. She met me at the bus station and looked every bit as good as she had a week before. She was tall, around five eleven, which was the same as me, and quite chubby in a good way. She had heart-melting pale blue eyes and favoured calf-length Laura Ashley dresses.

I thought we made a good couple, even though I had embraced the punk rock movement with enthusiasm, wearing an old suit I'd got at the Oxfam shop which was now covered in safety pins, together with a white shirt and narrow tie. I'd used about half a jar of Brylcreem on my hair, which was spiked up but smelled terrible. At one time I'd gone all the way and worn a ripped binliner and torn jeans for about two hours on the streets of Oxford, which is how long it took before someone punched me in the face. I decided to become more of an inner punk after that.

After exchanging polite greetings, we got into her Morris 1100 and Cathy gave me a guided tour of Milton Keynes, before taking me to her modest flat in the student part of town.

Over a meal of authentic Swiss fondue (she used real Swiss cheese), we talked about the weather, about living in Milton Keynes, about the people we both knew – everything except our passionate exchanges at the party the previous weekend. Her choice of music wasn't ideal – a punk rocker like me shouldn't really have been listening to the Blue Oyster Cult – but I was too scared to ask her to put something else on. Besides, I was quite enjoying it.

She politely asked about the football match I was so desperate to watch and I explained how I was in awe of Argentina, with their swaggering mustachioed conquistadors Kempes and Luque, their commanding centre-half Passarella and their midfield magician Ardiles. I was in full flow with the Argentina worship when I noticed the slightly glazed-over look on Cathy's face. It was quite apparent that she was regretting asking the question.

At 11.10 we moved into the living room and she turned on the TV. I opened the bottle of Blue Nun I'd brought with me and poured a couple of glasses, handing one to her.

This was make or break for Argentina. It was their World Cup Final, as one commentator said, not altogether accurately. They didn't just need to win against a strong Peru side, they needed to win by four goals or more to leapfrog Brazil at the top of the table and get through to the final.

David Coleman's disembodied voice bounced off a distant satellite, describing events a split second after they had happened on the screen. If he was excited, the home fans were in a state of delirium and the pitch was already covered in tickertape. I was sitting forward on the sofa, glass of Blue Nun in my hand, as the match got underway. Peru made the better start, hitting the post after a couple of minutes and following that with a header that missed the target by inches. 'What a let-off for Argentina!' screamed Coleman. 'A second chance goes a-begging.'

But that was the end of the Peruvian resistance. Mario Kempes, his long black hair flowing like a buccaneer's in the breeze, set the stadium alight with a fantastic dribble followed by an outrageous finish. The crowd went even more mad than before. Leopoldo Luque then hit the post, and Oscar Ortiz hit the bar. 'This time it's the bar,' said our commentator, evidently feeling the frustration as much as I was. The Argentina number 4 provided the comedy moment by tripping over his own feet, and Cathy asked who it was. Instead of just admitting that I didn't know, I launched into an unconvincing explanation that the lack of programme was to blame, as that was what serious football fans relied on to identify someone on the pitch.

Just before the break, the scoreline became 2–0 when left-back Alberto Tarantini headed home. And while the Argentina players, manager and crowd went berserk, Coleman kept an admirably cool head. 'According to my records,' he announced calmly, 'it's Tarantini's first goal for his country.'

I turned to Cathy and breathlessly went through what had happened in the first forty-five minutes, which was a fair indication that I still had quite a lot to learn about women. She cut me short by offering me a cup of coffee.

She was still in the kitchen when Kempes scored Argentina's third with his 'inevitable left foot' shortly after the restart, and the impossible suddenly seemed highly probable.

Minutes later, Luque's flamboyant diving header flew into an unguarded net and my wild whooping brought Cathy through, carrying two mugs, to see what was happening. It was the all-important fourth goal, prompting the excitable Argentina manager Cesar Luis Menotti to rush on to the pitch, the ever-present unfiltered cigarette glued to his lips.

There was no stopping the Argentinians now. Rene Houseman waltzed through the paper-thin defence for the fifth and Luque got the sixth. 'Oh, what finishing!' screamed Coleman just before the curtain came down on the most exciting, nail-biting, exhilarating, passionate game I had ever seen. I think the commentator felt the same way. There was ecstasy in his voice as he signed off from an 'absolutely jubilant Rosario'.

I never thought the day would come when I would rather be watching a match in Milton Keynes than South America, but thanks to the way I felt about Cathy, that day had come. This really was the best day of my life. An incredible game of foot-ball, and the woman I couldn't stop thinking about sitting beside me. I'd already started to fantasize about what it would be like living together, maybe even in Milton Keynes as I wouldn't want to interfere with her education.

I leaned over to kiss her, but she unexpectedly pulled away. I was stung, wondering how it could all have gone wrong so suddenly and without warning. Was it because I'd been so enthusiastic about the game and neglected her? Apparently not, as she then said the most heartbreaking words known to man:

'I really like you, but I think we should just be friends.'

'But what about last weekend?' I asked, my heart clinging on to the slenderest of hopes.

'We were both drunk,' she explained, as gently as she could.

I slept on the sofa, thinking of her a few feet away in her bed, possibly naked. It was torture, and I wondered how I could have gone from the highest high to the lowest low in such a short space of time. I woke up several times in the night, hoping that the whole thing (apart from the Argentina v. Peru match) had just been a bad dream.

Cathy woke me with toast and a cup of coffee at eight, and after we'd finished breakfast she drove me to the bus station in awkward silence. The atmosphere wasn't hostile; we just couldn't think of anything to say.

On the coach, I read several of the papers, happy that the reporters seemed to be as much in awe of the Argentina performance as I was. A couple did mention something I was unaware of: the Peruvian goalkeeper, known as 'El Loco', who had let in six goals, was in fact Argentinian. I put that to the back of my mind, unwilling to let any suspicions cloud my memory of such a brilliant match.

The next time I saw Cathy was two months later, which was almost but not quite enough time to get over the pain of that night. She was down in Wantage visiting her sister and dropped into the pub before going back to Milton Keynes. I was delighted to see her, and the hug she gave me made me think that maybe she had changed her mind, but my hopes were dashed when her sister mentioned that she was back with her old boyfriend. Cathy then took a large brown envelope out of her bag and handed it to me with a smile. Playing it cool, I thanked her and placed it on the seat beside me, not opening it until I got home later that night. As soon as I was indoors, I tore open the envelope and fished out a programme for Argentina v. Peru which she'd thoughtfully managed to get for me.

This was when I learned two things. That sometimes, friendship isn't such a bad consolation prize. And that the Argentina number 4 was called Daniel Bertoni.

Cathy and I stayed in touch, although our calls became less and less frequent. This was a shame on many levels, not the least of which was the fact that she would have almost certainly talked me out of what was about to happen next.

ARGYLE

THE OFFICIAL MATCH MAGAZINE OF PLYMOUTH ARGYLE FOOTBALL CLUB

Football League Division Three
Plymouth Argyle
v
Swindon Town
Saturday 16th September, 1978
Kick-off 3 pm   Match Magazine 20p

15

Plymouth Argyle v. Swindon Town, 16 September 1978

> The intense disappointment to the crowd in losing two successive home games is realised but it must be remembered that over the past two years morale at Home Park has been low.
>
> From the official match magazine

Dave and I were sitting in a particularly rough pub on the outskirts of Oxford, drinking Babycham, because that was what the dice had told us to do. We'd both recently read *The Dice Man* by Luke Rhinehart, a book about someone whose every decision was made on the roll of a dice, and being impressionable we had decided to live our lives the same way. Every time we had to decide anything, from what to eat to which film to watch, we'd write down six options and let the dice decide which one to take. This had its downside, which had never been more clearly illustrated than on the previous night, when we found ourselves in a near-empty cinema watching *The Magic of Lassie*, a seemingly endless musical about a kidnapped dog.

Trying to ignore the threatening glances from some of the building labourer types who were sitting at the nearest table (the cherries in our glasses probably didn't help), we laid out the sports page of the paper and studied the next day's football fixtures. The idea was to pick a game from each division, plus one from the Scottish Premier and First Divisions (Dave, being Scottish, insisted on these over my idea of Isthmian and Athenian League fixtures), then roll the dice to see which we'd be watching.

We were hoping for a One, which would mean a trip to Highbury for Arsenal v. Bolton, although a Two wouldn't be bad – a relatively short drive to Luton for their home game against Cardiff. A Three or Four would be dismal news, as neither Plymouth Argyle v. Swindon nor Reading v. Doncaster set the pulse racing. Even worse would be a Five or Six – at least a six-hour drive to witness either St Mirren v. Partick or Airdrie v. Raith Rovers.

The dice rattled across the mottled copper-covered table, before coming to a sticky halt in a small pool of Babycham. Three dots were face up. We would be going to Home Park in Plymouth. Not for the first time, I pondered the wisdom of this decision-making process.

We had to hitch to Plymouth. For once, we weren't doing something because the dice told us, we were doing it because we had no choice. We were both trying to save up for cars, so we were living on limited budgets and didn't want to blow several pounds on train fares. I'd be going as a Plymouth fan, because I had only recently begun to get over Swindon beating Bromley in the Cup two years earlier. I didn't know anything about Plymouth Argyle, apart from the fact that they played in green shirts and that Paul Mariner, the England centre-forward, used to play for them.

Fate was, for once, on our side and we got there in just a couple of hours. The first ride we got took us all the way to Plymouth and we had time to get some chips and take a leisurely walk through town before going to the match. I imagined that every single spectator had more rational reasons for being there than we did. And yet, there was something about Home Park that I fell in love with as soon as I got through the turnstile. It wasn't like other grounds the dice had taken us to. It had a friendly, welcoming feel, and I experienced the rare pleasure of thinking that the small wooden cube with dots had got it right.

The first thing to do when adopting a new team is to find a new hero. Rather than pass this responsibility over to the dice, we decided to use the more traditional method: find out who wears the number 9 shirt, and if he also happens to be top scorer, the search is over. In Plymouth's case, the same man filled both criteria. His name was Fred Binney, and if the number of homemade banners (HE'S NOT SKINNY, HE'S BINNEY) was anything to go by, he was perfect. I asked a couple of fans what he was like and the worship in their eyes told me more than mere words. They adored him. He was, I gathered, a bulky, wholehearted, heavily moustached centre-forward who, when he wasn't blasting shots into the stands, managed to score a fair few goals, usually either with his head or bundled in from a couple of yards out. One fan claimed that Binney had not only been signed by Brian Clough, he had also played alongside Pelé. I thought this was really stretching credibility but, bizarrely, both claims turned out to be true. He'd played for Brighton when Clough was in charge there, and for St Louis Stars in the US, outscoring Pelé when his team met the New York Cosmos.

Even though Binney had scored in the last couple of games, Plymouth's season was going downhill, with only one win in their last six games. They'd slid to fifteenth place in the table and crowd numbers were dropping. Today's attendance was definitely on the low side. I scoured the stands looking for

Plymouth's celebrity supporters, Michael Foot and the swimmer Sharron Davies, but neither appeared to be there.

As if to remind me that football and marching bands shared some unfathomable link, the teams came out to a tune I'd last heard being played by the Massed Bands of the Army's Junior Units at Wembley. My research, which consisted of asking the woman sitting next to me, revealed that it was called 'Semper Fidelis' and it wasn't just a piece of music, it was also the club's theme tune.

Fred Binney was an unmistakable figure, and the sight of him trundling around warmed my heart. He must have been in his early to mid thirties and was the antithesis of the well-tuned athlete I was used to seeing on TV, the kind of character you could only find in the lower divisions. His pre-match ritual clearly didn't include expending any energy, as he just stood around, taking the occasional lazy swing at any ball that happened to land in his vicinity. The Binney warm-up was a major influence on my own playing career and readily adopted by teammates in various hopeless Sunday League sides over the next decade or so.

The programme, or rather 'official match magazine of Plymouth Argyle Football Club', showed that Swindon had only two survivors from the team that had beaten Bromley 7–0, Steve Aizlewood and Kenny Stroud, which slightly lessened the hatred I harboured for them. One of my favourite things about programmes (or official match magazines) is the odd little things you pick up from them; in this case, the referee was a fingerprint expert, Argyle's Chris Harrison was a big fan of *The Good Life*, and Mr Hassan Habibi, from the P.A.S. club in Iran, would be watching his fourth successive Argyle home game today.

Page three was given over to manager Malcolm Allison, who wasn't happy with the way the crowd had booed his players in the last couple of games. He pleaded with the fans to 'get off the players' backs', adding, 'if you want to shout at anyone, shout at me – not the team'. Several fans behind the dugout took this advice to heart and gave him quite an earful as he took his place.

As the game got underway, it soon became apparent that the dice really had chosen well. It was a fast, skilful game with plenty of action at both ends.

Five minutes before the break, Brian Bason got the ball on halfway and beat a couple of Swindon defenders before chipping the ball over goalkeeper Chris Ogden from the edge of the area and into the net. This was not the kind of goal you expected to see in a Third Division match, and the reaction of the crowd around us let us know how special it was.

All we needed now was a Fred Binney goal to make the day complete.

He was looking dangerous, particularly in the second half, and had already had several chances. Then, on the hour, he was sent clear on goal, and showed surprising speed. But not quite enough, as Ogden sprinted out of his area to hoof the ball clear.

Twenty minutes later came the moment we'd been waiting for. Perrin hooked the ball over Ogden, leaving our hero to tap into an open goal from two yards out. We'd already begun celebrating when the great man scuffed his shot and it trickled harmlessly wide of the post.

A minute later, it was all forgotten. Binney fearlessly charged into the box and, despite being grabbed by Aizlewood, slid a low drive powerfully past Ogden. The crowd, including Dave and me, went berserk as Binney ran towards the fans, a huge beaming smile on his face and his arms spread in a 'how about *that*?' pose. They loved him. We loved him. So much so that after the final whistle we took up the invitation of two of the fans we were sitting with and went for a drink at the Pier West wine bar. Just so we could find out more about Fred Binney and the rest of the Argyle team.

We were surprised to learn that Malcolm Allison wasn't particularly popular because of what they saw as an overinflated opinion of himself. There was a feeling that as soon as a bigger club came along, he'd be off like a shot. I'd always thought he was a brilliant manager, but this was based more on his fondness for flamboyant fedora hats, Cuban cigars and oversized sheepskin coats than his achievements. Plus, how could anyone not admire a manager who was sacked from the very same job thirteen years earlier for sleeping with a director's wife? Apart from the director, obviously.

But at least some of Big Mal's players had made a positive impression on the fans. Apart from the great Fred Binney, the goalkeeper, Martin Hodge, was a real favourite, despite being only nineteen. We also discovered that Brian Bason's goal was the first by him that anyone could remember.

Inevitably we were asked what we were doing in Plymouth, and I was forced to explain. They seemed fascinated, and it wasn't long before the dice came out. Our newfound friends were instant converts and we spent an excellent evening drinking stout, cider and bloody Babycham with cherries. I got off lightly when it came to snacks, having to get pork scratchings, which I really liked. Dave wasn't so lucky, having to go up to the bar and order a beermat sandwich.

By the time we left the Pier West, cars were few and far between. The chances of two giggling men singing songs about Binney not being skinny getting a lift were slim at the best of times; at ten at night they were almost non-existent. The dice had a lot to answer for. When we eventually climbed into a beaten-up Morris 1100, the driver had clearly been drinking and it was almost a relief when he dropped us off in the middle of nowhere. We had eighty pence between us, nowhere to stay and no idea how we were going to get home.

It was too late and too dark to get a lift the rest of the way so we started walking in the direction of the nearest town, which was Bridgwater. As we were just about broke, we agreed, without consulting the dice, to try and get a bed at the police station by confessing to a series of unsolved crimes including hiding Lord Lucan and bumping off American union boss Jimmy Hoffa. The police were not amused and made us sit on hard wooden chairs in a draughty room. No tea, no biscuits, no comfy cell.

As the desk sergeant had counted on, we got bored and left, wandering around the deserted town until we came across an all-night launderette. We decided to spend the night there and make an early start the following morning. It was so cold that we took it in turns to put money into the drier and sit in front of it, occasionally opening the door to get a short-lived blast of warm air. We must have watched every minute pass on the wall clock; I have never known a night last so long. Around three a.m. I finally forced myself to question what I was doing there and whether it was really sensible to entrust everything to the throw of a dice. It was freezing, uncomfortable, and really, really boring. By the time daylight finally broke we'd run out of 10p pieces and were happy to begin the long walk to the M5, hoping to get a lift back to our nice, comfortable, fully heated house.

We did one last thing before leaving the launderette. On the small table that was used for magazines we left a small present for anyone who might be able to find a use for them: two well-worn white dice with black spots.

I'd had enough of a life that seemed to consist mainly of doing stupid things. I was twenty-three years old, and it was time to grow up.

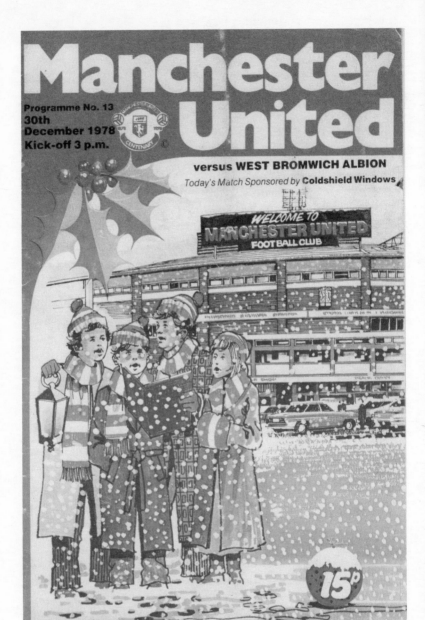

Manchester United

Programme No. 13
30th December 1978
Kick-off 3 p.m.

versus WEST BROMWICH ALBION

Today's Match Sponsored by **Coldshield Windows**

WELCOME TO MANCHESTER UNITED FOOTBALL CLUB

15p

16

Manchester United v. West Bromwich Albion, 30 December 1978

A feature of the Throstles' play has been the exciting attacking skills of their coloured forwards Cyrille Regis and Laurie Cunningham who have hit well over 20 goals between them.

From the official programme

Although the Gardeners' house still looked the same, their causes had changed in the twelve years since my last visit to Manchester. There were now posters in their front window for the Right to Work movement, the Socialist Workers Party and the Anti-Nazi League, of which I had become a member after seeing Paul Weller from The Jam and Joe Strummer from The Clash wearing ANL badges in the *NME*. Another poster protested about battery farming, and there was something about the Shah of Iran, although I couldn't work out if they were for or against him.

I was in Manchester for a New Year's Eve party, which was being held by a student friend of Dave's who had guaranteed that there would be wall-to-wall women. Despite being twenty-three, I was still naive enough to believe such claims and was really looking forward to it, even though I was slightly unsure what I would do when faced with wall-to-wall women. But before the party I planned to visit Old Trafford, for Manchester United's game with West Bromwich, an important fixture as both sides had a realistic chance of winning the league. I couldn't face sleeping on Dave's friend's floor so I'd asked my mum to ask the Gardeners if they could put me up, and they'd agreed.

Over lunch, which was cold leftovers from their Christmas nut roast with cranberries, I learned that Paul (or Pahl as I thought he was called), the friend I'd made when I was eleven, was no longer in the area. I gathered that he'd got himself into some pretty serious trouble in his late teens and had spent time in prison; they'd lost track of him after that. This saddened me and made me feel guilty about stopping sending him programmes.

I had hoped to persuade Simon, the youngest of the Gardeners still living at home and a United fan, to come to the game with me, but he had other things to do. I suspected that included watching the big Honey Boy Zimba v. John Elijah wrestling clash on TV, with the equally appetizing bout between Johnny England and Ringo Rigby also on the bill. It was a shame he couldn't make it. I never really enjoyed going on my own, especially on cold, frosty afternoons like this – thirty games had already been postponed and the Pools Panel were standing by. I'd applied to join them once, when I was at school, but had never got a reply.

There was one player I was desperate to see. I prided myself in my ability to spot a superstar of the future, and this eighteen-year-old was going to be one. His name was Andy Ritchie and he was an England youth international who had scored in both the games he'd stood in for Joe Jordan. It felt good knowing I was in on the beginning of something special.

Going to Old Trafford was like going home, even though I'd never been there before. I'd spent much of my adolescence fantasizing that I was watching George Best, Denis Law and Bobby Charlton playing in front of their home crowd and the pitch itself was familiar as I'd seen it many times on *Match of the Day*. The first sighting of the WELCOME TO MANCHESTER UNITED FOOTBALL CLUB sign made the hairs on my arms stand up.

My first stop was the Red Devils' souvenir shop. I remembered being impressed that Swindon had sold nearly thirty different items, as opposed to Bromley's paltry three; Manchester United put this into perspective by announcing that they had over two hundred lines 'including many Centenary commemorative items'. This was a truly big club.

The programme was just as impressive. I loved the colourful festive cover, which showed a poorly drawn family warmly wrapped in red and white scarves, singing carols in front of the ground as the snow gently fell – an image slightly more reassuring than the reality, which was the solid mass of shaven-headed youths, also in United scarves, who I'd noticed milling around in roughly the same area.

I spent the twenty minutes before kick-off devouring this programme from cover to cover, barely able to believe that I was sitting in Manchester United's ground, in Stand E, which was the best I could afford, given that I still had to buy a bottle of cider for the party. I was relieved when I read that Paddy Mulligan, West Brom's signing from Crystal Palace, had been left out. The last time I'd seen him, back in the Mandy days, he'd torn United's defence to pieces. I was also happy to see Cyrille Regis in their side, as he had been signed from the Isthmian League, where Bromley played.

The adverts were of a much higher standard than most of the other programmes in my collection. One that had me nodding my head in admiration was for the *Manchester Evening News* Pink edition, which carried the results every Saturday after the game. THE REDS IN THE PINK read the brilliant headline. When I turned the page to the 'Your Letters' section, I was stunned to see a penpal request from someone in South Africa whose name was Pahl.

While it was exciting watching the United team run out in the swirling snow, it was especially thrilling to see Andy Ritchie in the flesh. You could tell in the warm-up that he was really special, as he blasted shots past Gary Bailey with effortless ease. It was hard to believe that he was five years younger than me and I felt that Tony Godden in the Albion goal would be in for a tough day. Albion also had a young player who was meant to be quite good, Bryan Robson, but he hadn't made anywhere near the same impression when I'd seen him on *Match of the Day*. The main danger, I felt sure, would come from Regis, Laurie Cunningham and Brendan Batson. Together they were known as The Three Degrees, because they were black and because there were three of them.

I'd never seen a black English player before, except on TV, and even that was a rarity. The most famous was probably Viv Anderson, who had just made his England debut against Czechoslovakia. I was excited by their presence in the game and felt proud of the way football was helping to unite black and white in the same way that the Rock Against Racism concerts had brought people together over music.

The ground was packed and the atmosphere so intense that I felt a little light-headed. In the first attack, virtually from the kick-off, Regis bore in on goal and scuffed his shot. There was a scattering of boos for the Albion striker, I assumed because he had nearly scored. Batson got the same reaction minutes later, when his diving header, following a well-worked free kick, went only just wide of Bailey's post.

I didn't give it any thought as the action moved to the other end. United were gradually getting on top and deservedly took the lead when a Sammy McIlroy corner was headed away to Brian Greenhoff on the edge of the area. The blond-haired midfielder hit a first-time volley into the roof of the net for a goal that was so good, he looked as though he could scarcely believe it.

Almost from the restart, Cunningham went on a run down the left and this time the booing was more audible. There were also animal sounds coming from the paddocks in front of me and behind the goal. Several United fans were gesturing angrily towards the winger, who must have felt a small level of satisfaction when the cross was converted by Tony Brown into the far corner to make it 1–1. This seemed to incense some sections of the crowd even more and shouting was now coming from spectators near where I was sitting.

This wasn't the usual abuse directed at the opposition's best player, this was hatred of someone because of the colour of his skin. The realization momentarily stunned me, as it was something I'd never experienced before.

Suddenly afraid of what might happen if the wrong person saw it, I instinctively moved my hand to cover the Anti-Nazi League badge on my lapel, before taking it off and putting it safely in the pocket of my bomber jacket. I'd never been particularly brave.

It seemed a wise decision a few minutes later. With the snow falling hard, Cunningham went on a run past several defenders and caressed the ball to Regis, who backheeled it into the path of Cantello. The midfielder finished beautifully from the edge of the area for one of the best goals I'd ever seen. It certainly deserved more than the near silence that greeted it.

Albion's lead was short-lived, however. From a Houston free kick, Gordon McQueen rose unchallenged and headed past

Godden for the equalizer. Andy Ritchie attempted to envelop the scorer in a bear hug – his first meaningful contribution to the game.

And the goals refused to dry up after that. It was Sammy McIlroy's turn next, as he got the ball on the edge of the area on his left foot, switched to his right and hit an unstoppable shot to make it 3–2.

When Cunningham went to fetch the ball for a throw-in not long after, I saw fans spitting in his direction and screaming insults. It was happening directly in front of me and was by far the worst thing I'd seen at a football match. Even though I'd come to the game wanting United to win, I now wanted to see Cunningham, Regis and Batson have the games of their lives, to show that unlike me they weren't going to be intimidated.

That was when I decided, in my own small way, that I was going to make a statement of support. Realizing that it should be more than a fashion accessory, I nervously took the Anti-Nazi League badge from my pocket and, with a shaking hand, pinned it back on to my lapel.

No one noticed, but it made me feel as though I was making a stand.

Not long after that, Tony Brown finished a flowing move by prodding home a Cantello flick on, and it was 3–3. This was the last action of the first half, which had been a stunning forty-five minutes of football. The rest of the crowd seemed just as impressed, giving the teams a standing ovation.

The action didn't let up in the second half – a Robinson header was cleared off the line by Brian Greenhoff, Gary Bailey made an incredible diving save from Regis, and Allie Brown had the miss of the season by blasting over from two yards out. Luckily, the abuse had faded by then, as though the sting had been taken out of the more hostile elements of the Old Trafford crowd.

Albion scored twice in the closing stages, and the black players were at the heart of both goals. For the fourth, Regis flicked on a long ball into the path of Cunningham, who advanced on Bailey before slotting comfortably past him for his eleventh of season. Then, with time almost up, came another goal of breathtaking brilliance. Cunningham outpaced Houston on the right and passed inside to Brown, who supplied Regis with a half chance that he gleefully converted. His beaming smile gave me a feeling of satisfaction, even though he'd just made sure my team were well beaten.

I made my way back to the Gardeners' with a new appreciation of the work they did for various causes and promised myself that I'd do more in future than just wear badges and T-shirts with slogans. When I packed my bag the following morning, I took a small stack of leaflets and booklets which I was going to work my way through once I got home. I felt as though I was finally growing up.

That afternoon I watched the game again on *Kick Off*, the local version of *The Big Match*, while we were supposed to be getting Dave's friend's flat ready for the party. There was no mention of the spitting and booing whenever one of the black players touched the ball, which surprised me. It was only later that I realized it was nothing out of the ordinary, and they probably had to put up with it every week.

They'd definitely made their mark on this game, however. The West Brom manager Ron Atkinson, in patent leather overcoat, praised the contribution of 'the coloured lads' while commentator Elton Welsby finished his piece by saying that 'the magic the black players are bringing to football was completely in evidence'.

The party that night, unlike the match, failed to live up to expectations. There really were lots of women. Not that it made any difference to me. I ended up talking to an art director with a local advertising agency, as we were both too shy to approach anyone else. He wasn't even interested in football, so the conversation was limited to things earnest young men at parties were prone to discussing with each other, like Anti-Nazi League gigs, how much we'd donated to the Sid Vicious Defence Fund, whether *NME* should really be reviewing the Grateful Dead album, and how Thatcher would destroy Britain if she ever got into power. I think he was as bored with me as I was with him, as we both kept glancing around, hoping for one of the wall-to-wall women to come over and sweep us away. By the time the midnight hour struck I'd long given up hope of a New Year snog, but I managed to make a New Year's resolution, which was to get a proper job, as the signs were that if the Conservatives got in, the MG factory would be closed down. I also decided to get a serious long-term girlfriend, mainly because all my friends had one.

The first resolution took six months to happen, when, inspired by my fellow partygoer, I landed a job in Leeds as a trainee copywriter with 'the North's leading advertising agency' after seeing an ad in *Campaign*, the trade magazine. I was sad to leave Wantage and the MG factory behind, but it was time for a fresh start.

Besides, I thought I had a better chance of making the second resolution happen in a place where I didn't already know everyone.

LEEDS UNITED

OFFICIAL MATCH DAY PROGRAMME   PRICE 20p   No.19

FOOTBALL LEAGUE DIVISION ONE   SATURDAY 17th MARCH, 1979

LIVERPOOL

In This Issue . . .

Jimmy Adamson on United's get-away break in Spain.

Spotlight man Kevin Hird says thanks for the welcome.

News about Eddie Gray's big night, United's Top Fan from Merseyside, our new fixture dates, plus a welcome to the men from Anfield.

17

Leeds United v. Liverpool,
17 May 1979

Tonight we welcome the new league champions Liverpool to
Elland Road to round off the season here on a high note.

From the official programme

I was literally shaking with nerves as I sat on the bus to Elland
Road, where Leeds were taking on Liverpool in the last game
of the season. The reason for my anxiety was simple: if Leeds
won, there was a serious possibility that I would be homeless.

A combination of Yorkshire Bitter, an overloud jukebox and
an inflated opinion of my football expertise was to blame.
Twenty-four hours earlier I'd been in the Highlander, a pub
opposite the office, having a quiet after-work drink with a few
of my colleagues. There was a clear demarcation: the account
directors, in their suits and ties, sat on one side of the table,
while us creative types, who shunned such conformity, sat on
the other side in our black T-shirts and jeans. Being right next
to the jukebox meant sometimes having to shout to be heard, an
action which could, under the wrong circumstances, be mis-
interpreted as an act of belligerence. So later in the evening,

when I, desperate to make my point over Earth, Wind and Fire's 'Boogie Wonderland', loudly proclaimed that the current Liverpool side fully deserved to beat Leeds' record points tally, which would happen when they beat Leeds in the final game of the season, it didn't go down well with Jim, a passionate Leeds fan sitting opposite.

He slammed his pint of Yorkshire Bitter down and shouted back, despite the fact that the song had finished, that there was no way they'd win and I should put my money where my mouth was. The problem was that I had hardly any money, and even if I had I wouldn't have put it on a bet I had every likelihood of losing. It soon became obvious that cashflow wasn't a problem for him. 'Fifty quid says you're wrong,' he said, getting his stuffed wallet out and removing five crisp ten-pound notes, which he placed on the table in front of me.

Fifty quid? The biggest bet I'd ever had was fifty pence, and that was on Andy Pandy to win the Grand National a couple of years before. He fell over early in the race and Red Rum, whom Dave and everyone else had said would win, won. After that, I promised myself I'd never make a stupid bet again. A promise I was about to break. 'You're on,' I said angrily, stung by the fact that my football judgement was being questioned, even though I had the sneaky feeling that he might actually know what he was talking about, having seen every Leeds home game that season. 'You can have the draw,' I added, with the kind of confidence and generosity that only comes from too much alcohol.

Giving him the draw was an even more pointless gesture considering the fact that £50 probably isn't much money when you're a Porsche-driving advertising executive with a detached house in Guiseley; for a carless junior copywriter it was a month's rent. Which I wouldn't be able to pay if I lost the bet. I'd only just moved into a really nice flat in Roundhay with a bearded scientist (who I knew I wouldn't get on with) and a pretty waitress (who I desperately hoped I would). My room was a large one on the top floor. I had managed to acquire a gigantic six-sheet Heineken poster from work that showed Mr Spock from *Star Trek* having his pointy ears refreshed by the beer that refreshed the parts other beers could not reach, and this covered three walls, including, inconveniently, the light switch. And now I could lose it all because of an idiotic bet, which stemmed from me passionately defending Liverpool, a team I had no particular feelings for.

When the bus pulled up outside Elland Road, I got off and walked the rest of the way to the ground. The last time I'd been there, for the Southampton game a few months earlier, rubbish had been piled high in the surrounding streets, as dustmen and pretty much everyone except copywriters had been on strike. Being an ardent socialist (even if I wasn't quite sure what one was), I fully supported all industrial action, apart from the time Yorkshire TV's Sunday afternoon *Football Special* was taken off air for a couple of weeks. That had made me really angry.

It was an all-ticket game, and the ground was absolutely packed. There was a true end-of-term feel and I'd been really lucky to get a ticket for the K Stand, where I had a very good view of the corner flag. The programme was an odd one. It had been produced for 17 March, when the fixture was originally due to be played before being postponed. The club had come up with the brilliant idea of selling this with a four-page black-and-white insert inside that contained 'up to date news plus a look back on the season by Jimmy Adamson'. This was a first for my collection.

The programme seemed to be filled with taunting reminders of my predicament: a man who'd picked up £1,000 in the Leeds United Lottery was pictured clutching a bunch of fivers, an advert from the Yorkshire Bank promised personal loans so customers could 'make marvellous improvements to their home', and some blurb for the Golden Goal competition promised £120 to the winner, noting that goals would be timed using watches supplied by Owen and Robinson of Albion Street.

I'd been so worried about the outcome of the match at work that instead of writing about why WASS commercial vehicles were superior I'd come up with a list of Good Signs – 1. Liverpool already champions; 2. Kenny Dalglish Footballer of the Year; 3. Best defence in the league; 4. Leeds' best player, Tony Currie, out injured – and Bad Signs – 1. Liverpool already champions, so may not try so hard; 2. Leeds held them at Anfield; 3. Leeds desperate to avoid losing their record of sixty-seven points in a season; 4. Leeds good enough to qualify for Europe; 5. Leeds at home; 6. Leeds have the incentive of needing a win to clinch fourth place; 7. Leeds' Player of the Year is their goalkeeper David Harvey and I can't win the bet unless Liverpool score at least once – and, ominously, the Bad Signs list was much longer.

I had another to add when the teams came out. The Leeds players formed a guard of honour to welcome my new favourite team on to the pitch. I felt this was a psychological ploy that had clearly been designed to remind Liverpool that they were already champions and didn't have anything to prove. I got even more worried when Phil Thompson took his team down to the Kop End, where they received rapturous applause. Didn't he realize that this would make them feel complacent? What sort of captain was he?

Every time the ball went into the Liverpool half I felt on the verge of a nervous breakdown; when they managed to get anywhere near Ray Clemence's goal, I shut my eyes in fear, feeling vast waves of relief wash over me when sounds of disappointment came from the home supporters, especially when John

Hawley must have only just missed. I knew this because when I opened my eyes he was clutching his head in anguish and Eddie Gray was giving him a consoling pat on the back.

Then, after twenty minutes, my anxiety levels rocketed when Liverpool scored. The in-form David Johnson clearly fouled Paul Hart, but the referee, Mr J. Hunting of Leicester, waved play on. The ball found its way to Terry McDermott, whose shot was well saved by Harvey, but Johnson followed up to slot the ball home. My heart was thumping and my breathing became shallow as I tried to contain the excitement. There were still seventy minutes left and I was convinced that the linesman would tell the ref about Johnson's foul at half time, and he would then retroactively disallow the goal.

That's the kind of paranoia that enters your mind when fifty quid is at stake.

I needed another goal before the break, although it would take a four- or five-goal cushion before I could start thinking about relaxing. Peeking through my fingers, I watched as an Arthur Graham shot flew harmlessly over the bar. If it had been about four yards lower, it could have cost me a week's wages.

Leeds were looking likely to score every time they got the ball. Well, to me they were anyway. But then, just before the break, Jimmy Case struck a fierce shot that gave Harvey no chance. To the people standing alongside me, the game was effectively over. To me, Liverpool were in big trouble. Everyone knows that 2–0 is the worst lead you can have. All it takes is for the other side to pull a goal back and suddenly you're faced with the scores being level.

When the whistle blew for half time I tried to take my mind off what was unfolding on the pitch by focusing on the programme. I had been intrigued by the Leeds fans' habit of sending in heartfelt poems to the Fans Forum page, and today there was yet another one. Gill Hall's verse to Tony Currie resonated with me because it reminded me of the poems I used to compose for my heroes, although mine were never published. 'Tony's brains are in his feet,' went Gill's poem. 'He moves so fast but oh so neat. When he scores, I jump from my seat.' It took me back to a time when I'd get hugely excited about rhyming a few words about players ranging from George Best of Manchester United to Alan Stonebridge of Bromley.

The second half almost started catastrophically. Eddie Gray, who had looked dangerous in patches, played a brilliant pass through to Carl Harris, who was left with the simple task of lobbing the ball over the advancing Clemence for his sixth goal of the season. This time I couldn't close my eyes. Instead I watched, at first in horror as Harris lined up his shot, then in disbelief as he tamely prodded it straight at the goalkeeper.

When Liverpool added a third soon after that, again through David Johnson, I thought about writing him a thank you letter, but decided it would probably be a bit weird. Instead, I made the mistake of relaxing. I was soon reminded that the game wasn't yet over when a Hawley thunderbolt was tipped over the bar by Ray Clemence, my new favourite goalie. I was almost beginning to believe that Leeds couldn't score three times in the last two minutes, although deep down I felt that they probably would.

I counted down the seconds on my watch, and after a totally unjustified and agonizing thirty-seven seconds of injury time, Mr Hunting finally blew his whistle and I was fifty pounds richer.

If I'd been able to see the game through the eyes of a football fan as opposed to a paranoid and reckless gambler, I would've appreciated just how good Liverpool were. Dalglish controlled everything, Johnson provided speed and accuracy, while McDermott, Case and Kennedy combined tireless running with sublime touches. They played with calmness, grace and assurance, and earned a massive ovation from the locals.

If taxi fares hadn't gone up so much recently because of the Iran oil crisis, I would've gone home in style to celebrate a huge win for me and Liverpool. Instead, I got the bus and allowed myself just one small indulgence – a box of forty-eight packets of Walker's cheese and onion crisps from the shop on the corner.

The next morning I was half expecting Jim to try and get out of paying, but he came down and handed over the money just after I'd sat down at my desk.

'Here you go,' he said, with the indifferent tone of someone handing over a box of matches rather than a small fortune. 'You must have been worried for a while there.'

'Me, worried? Not at all,' I lied. 'I said Liverpool would win, didn't I?'

It felt brilliant having fifty pounds in my wallet, having never had so much in my life. But winning is only truly satisfying when you have someone to share it with. And I hadn't had a girlfriend in months.

Something that was about to change in the most unexpected way.

LEEDS
UNITED

OFFICIAL MATCH DAY
PROGRAMME No. 10
PRICE 25p

UEFA CUP
2nd Round/2nd Leg
Wed. 7th November, 1979

LEEDS
IN
EUROPE

**UNIVERSITATEA
CRAIOVA**
(Rumania)

18

Leeds United v. Universitatea Craiova,
7 November 1979

Although our knowledge of the Rumanian language made it
difficult to get to grips with the article [in the programme for
the away leg] there were several mentions of Mick Jagger, Peter
Frampton, Rick Wakeman and Paul Simon and their interest in
soccer in the States.

From the official programme

When you thought about European football in the late
seventies, the giants of the game came to mind: Juventus, with
superstars like Marco Tardelli and Dino Zoff; the St Etienne
side that boasted Michel Platini and Johnny Rep; Valencia with
Mario Kempes; and Karl-Heinz Rummenigge's Bayern
Munich.

What didn't spring into your head was Universitatea Craiova
of Romania.

But they were the reason I was at a sparsely populated Elland
Road on a cold, wet Wednesday night in November for a UEFA
Cup match with Bob, an art director from work. We'd bonded
almost from the day he started, as we both had an interest in

football that bordered on obsession. His favourite fact was that Leeds could field an entire team of players with surnames beginning with H. As I looked at the line-ups, I wondered if somewhere in Craiova someone was equally proud that their team could field a side whose surnames ended in U. It was unlikely.

We'd decided to go to the game for a couple of reasons. Firstly, it had the potential to be an exciting one, with Leeds needing to attack to make up the two-goal deficit from the first leg. The other factor was a rumour Bob had heard about the Leeds players going to a club in town called the Nouveau after midweek matches. Bob and I had decided to go there too, although it wasn't clear what we'd do if we saw any of the players. Stare at them, probably.

Tonight's programme had provided me with one invaluable piece of information, which I'd filed away for later. In his column 'Captain's Corner', Trevor Cherry revealed that he was a fan of Alistair MacLean's novels. I'd recently finished *Ice Station Zebra*, so I'd have something to talk to him about if I accidentally bumped into him at the Nouveau, even though I hadn't really managed to follow the plot.

But before we could all go clubbing, there was the small matter of seeing off Craiova. Leeds had been so poor all season that neither of us was convinced they could win – and judging by the small attendance, neither did the Leeds public. They were just above the relegation zone, and Bob and I had witnessed them lose to Bristol City the previous Saturday, in a season when very few teams lost to Bristol City.

Just before the teams appeared, the ground announcer asked for silence while a police message was played over the Tannoy. Much to my surprise, the fans in the notorious Gelderd End seemed to respect this request, as an eerie quiet enveloped the ground. Maybe they're not really that bad, I thought. Then came the plea: 'If anyone recognizes the voice you're about to hear, please let the police know.'

There was then a gap of a few seconds as they cued up the tape. Then it began.

'I'm Jack,' came the sound of a familiar Geordie accent. 'I see you are still having no luck catching me. I have the greatest respect for you, George, but oh Lord! You are no nearer catching me.'

The Yorkshire Ripper's voice still sent a shiver through me, even though, like most people living in the area, I'd heard this cassette he'd sent to George Oldfield, head of the Ripper inquiry, countless times.

My admiration for the Leeds fans' public spirit vanished as the rest was drowned out by the fans behind the goal singing 'One Yorkshire Ripper, there's only one Yorkshire Ripper'. Not for the first time, I was witnessing the less pleasant side of humanity at a football ground.

What followed was almost as soul-destroying. After having finished the 1978/79 season in fifth place with exciting attacking football, Leeds were going through a terrible patch, undeserving of the fantastic support they were given by increasingly small crowds. The previous season's twenty-seven-goal strike partnership of Hawley and Currie had gone and manager Jimmy Adamson had replaced them with a former right-back, Trevor Cherry, and a goal-shy striker, Ray Hankin. They were so short of ideas and so reliant on set-pieces that their top scorer was centre-half Paul Hart. And it was Hart who almost provided the perfect start. I'd barely had time to put the programme in my pocket before, unbelievably, he missed with a header from a few yards out.

There are few worse things in football than watching a toothless attack up against a ten-man defence, but that pretty much summed up the first half. The only light relief for the home fans had come when the announcer gamely attempted to read out the Craiova line-up. Some things just aren't meant to be attempted with a Yorkshire accent, and the names 'Sorin Cirtu' and 'Aurel Beldeanu' are two of them.

In the programme, Maurice Lindsay, the assistant manager, had prepared a detailed 'Spy file on Craiova', which had involved him sneaking over the border from Yugoslavia with the Leeds chief scout to watch their away game with Baia Mare. It was like something out of an Alistair MacLean novel, although I suspected Lindsay wasn't quite cut out for the cloak-and-dagger life as he appeared to have got the names of several Craiova players wrong in his dossier. Sorin Cirtu had become Sdrian Cirtu, while Aurel Beldeanu's name had changed to Anrika Beldeanu.

Perhaps if his attention to detail had been better these two might not have got on the scoresheet late in the second half to give Craiova a deserved 2–0 win on the night and a 4–0 victory on aggregate. Cirtu's goal came via a cruel deflection off Byron Stevenson that wrongfooted John Lukic, but Beldeanu's was the best I'd seen at Elland Road all season, an unstoppable shot from thirty yards out to ensure his side went into the draw for the next round alongside teams like Bayern Munich, Feyenoord and St Etienne.

Outside the ground a crowd had assembled, and they weren't happy. Several hundred disgruntled fans were chanting 'We want football!' and 'Adamson out!' After what I'd just gone through I was tempted to join them, but we had pressing business at the Nouveau. I hoped none of the protesters were going there. I wanted the Leeds players to be relaxed.

We took the bus into town and got off at Briggate, the main street in the city centre. The Nouveau was above a pub called the Brahms and Liszt, and I'd never been there before. In fact I'd never been to any club in Leeds before, but since I'd observed on more than one occasion that Bob had the enviable ability to approach anyone he fancied and talk to them, I'd gone along with his idea. This meant I'd be forced to abandon my usual strategy of standing around, drink in hand, coolly assessing the women until it was time to go home on my own.

It didn't take Bob long to make his move. As 'I Will Survive' by Gloria Gaynor was finishing, he elbowed me in the ribs and nodded towards a table where a couple of girls in their early twenties were sitting. Both had long brown hair and were exceptionally pretty. Bob strode over confidently; I followed at a distance so I could make a detour and pretend I wasn't interested if he got rejected.

But whatever he said seemed to go down well.

He waved me over and introduced me to Lynn and Caroline. We talked about what we did for a living and found out that they were both nurses who had come straight from finishing the evening shift. They weren't as impressed as I'd hoped when I casually mentioned that we worked in advertising. Then, as 'Heart of Glass' by Blondie started, Bob grabbed Lynn and led her over to the dance floor. 'Oh, I love this record,' said Caroline, which I interpreted as 'I wish you'd ask me to dance', so I asked her if she wanted to dance. She agreed, although I found out later that she had in fact only meant that she loved the record.

My dancing technique consisted of standing on the spot looking down and shifting from foot to foot, swaying self-consciously while twisting my upper body slightly from one side to the other, my arms bent horizontally, in a Popeye pose. Still, at least it would be over in four minutes and then we could sit down again. Or so I thought. The DJ had apparently thought it a good idea to play the twelve-inch version, which lasted almost twice as long and made me increasingly aware of just how repetitive my dance moves were.

When it finally came to an end, he made an announcement. He asked us all to listen carefully to the tape he was about to play and if anyone recognized the voice they were to call their local police. Then the Ripper tape was played for the second time that evening. Just as at Elland Road, everyone stopped what they were doing and listened. And afterwards the atmosphere changed slightly: there was less laughter and the chatter was more subdued. This is what tends to happen when you hear the taunting, boastful voice of a man claiming to be responsible for at least eleven murders.

When the music started up again, Bob and Lynn, who were all over each other, returned to the dance floor. Caroline and I reached an unspoken agreement not to follow suit. Instead, we finally found common ground, inspired by what we'd just heard. The Yorkshire Ripper. She told me how she'd been on duty when one of his victims was brought into casualty. They'd managed to save her life and Caroline had looked after her during her recovery. Since the murders began, the hospital had provided taxis to and from work, and nurses were encouraged to go everywhere in pairs. Which was why she'd agreed to come along to the Nouveau with Lynn tonight.

I then told her of my slightly more tenuous link to the case. The agency Bob and I worked for had recently done a series of high-profile ads which were launched in a blaze of publicity; the claim was that it was 'a million-pound campaign', even though everyone seemed to contribute their time and resources for nothing. There were posters everywhere saying HELP US STOP THE RIPPER FROM KILLING AGAIN, and asking passers-by to look at the handwriting from a letter he'd sent to George Oldfield and to ring (0532) 464111 and listen to the tape. Although I hadn't technically been involved in creating the poster, I was in the same building at the time, which I felt counted for something.

After that, we both seemed to relax. She even showed an interest in the programme I produced from my pocket, in answer to her question about what we'd been up to before coming to the Nouveau. I drew her attention to an article about David Harvey's long-term hamstring injury, but she was unable to provide any fresh medical insights into how long he would be out for.

At some stage that evening I realized I was no longer glancing at the club entrance, hoping to catch a glimpse of Leeds footballers coming in. Instead I was lost in conversation, enjoying Caroline's company and hoping she wouldn't start yawning and looking at her watch.

As it was going so well, I asked her if she wanted to come for a walk on Sunday afternoon. It would mean missing the eagerly awaited clash between Luton Town and QPR on TV, but I sensed it would be worth it. And it was. Afterwards, we went for a meal at the Flying Pizza, which was in no way influenced by the fact that Leeds legend Allan 'Sniffer' Clarke was supposed to be a regular there, according to an advert in a recent programme.

Not long after that, Bob and Lynn's brief romance may have been over but ours was destined for bigger and better things. Meeting Caroline's parents was next up, and I was thrilled to discover they lived a short drive from Plymouth Argyle's Home Park. Three months later I moved in with her, and it was clear to both of us that we'd found what we were looking for. Less than a football season later, we were engaged.

CHELSEA

NORTHWICH VICTORIA
v OR
WIGAN ATHLETIC

SEASON 1979–80

**F.A. CUP
3rd ROUND**
Saturday January 5
3pm

OFFICIAL PROGRAMME

25p

OUR NEXT HOME MATCH IS THE BIG ONE!

It's Chelsea v Newcastle here next Saturday

19

Chelsea v. Northwich Victoria or Wigan Athletic, 5 January 1980

This is the first time we have produced a match programme showing two possible opponents, and whichever of those clubs has come through, we warmly welcome them.

From the official programme

I was sitting in a West London film studio watching a dozen actor types milling around, each reading the script I'd written, practising their inflections and wide-eyed sincerity, repeating lines over and over again. They looked pretty much the same – sharp suits, gleaming white teeth, bland good looks. Only one of them deviated from this, a slightly scruffy unshaven figure who bore a startling resemblance to George Best.

I kept glancing at my watch, fidgeting. Even though I was thrilled to be casting my first ever TV commercial, which we'd be shooting the next day, my priority now was quickly agreeing on the perfect spokesman for WASS Used Cars (Leeds) Ltd, then getting to Stamford Bridge for the FA Cup tie between Chelsea and Wigan.

This was a game I was desperate to see. My biggest regret in football was turning down the chance to go to Stamford Bridge the week after watching Bromley put ten past the Civil Service in 1971. If I'd taken Dave up on the offer, I would have witnessed Chelsea beating Jeunesse Hautcharage 13–0 in a European Cup Winners' Cup game. Statistically, this would have put me in an elite group. How many other collectors could boast programmes from consecutive matches with double-digit scorelines? It was something I tried not to think about.

But now there was a chance of redemption. While free-scoring Chelsea, profiting from a mix of showmanship and adventure, were top of the Second Division, Wigan, who had only recently joined the Football League, were stuck halfway down the Fourth. They'd only got past Northwich Victoria after a replay, so there was a chance of seeing plenty of goals – maybe even another ten – during my London trip, as well as covering myself in advertising glory.

The commercial's director and I sat down at a table, and the auditions started. I soon started to get impatient. Not only did the candidates all look and sound the same, but I needed to get it over and done with, as the game would be kicking off in under an hour. And then the George Best lookalike entered the room. It soon became evident that the similarities were more than physical. When he started reading for us, he revealed a strong Irish accent:

'When it comes to used cars, you can't go past Wass,' he said, pronouncing the name 'Wuss'. 'They have excellent deals on many popular models and stand behind each car. So if you need a used car, call Wass today.'

I felt a stirring of excitement. I saw myself as a maverick, someone who was going to change the face of advertising. And this was where the revolution was going to start. I was determined to use a real person in my ads, not some clone in a suit. I noticed that the director had put a big cross next to his name. I put a big tick.

I kept glancing at my watch, getting increasingly anxious as kick-off time approached while I was stuck in a small room with a bunch of actors desperate for their fifteen seconds of fame. I turned to the director and said, 'Let's go with the Irish bloke.' He looked at me in shock, but to avoid having to discuss it I gathered my papers and ran out of the door.

I got to Stamford Bridge a few minutes before kick-off and quickly bought a programme from a glove-wearing seller. I liked that – it eliminated the chance of smearing or finger-prints, ensuring pristine condition. Which had never been more important, since he'd handed me the most unusual pro-gramme I was ever likely to see.

Like me, it broke all the rules. I gaped, open-mouthed in astonishment, at what I was seeing. For the first time in my twenty-four years I was looking at a programme where the home team had two opponents. On the cover it said Chelsea v. Northwich Victoria or Wigan Athletic; on the back, it listed all three teams. This was unprecedented. I bought a further five copies. The extra £1.25 didn't matter – I'd put it on expenses, even though the seller was unable to give me a receipt.

The theme of uncertainty ran throughout the programme. There were team profiles on both Northwich Victoria and Wigan, and it was bizarre to think that Northwich, the team with the programme's most interesting profile, wouldn't be playing. Their ranks included a goalkeeper who dyed curtains for a living, a frozen food manufacturer and a couple of teachers. The most interesting thing about Wigan, and it really wasn't terribly interesting, was that both of their goalkeepers were struggling with cartilage injuries.

I was still trying to digest the whole three teams/one pro-gramme thing as I went through the turnstiles. It could only have happened because Chelsea's opponents had been decided just a few days earlier, when Wigan finally got past Northwich following four postponements, one abandoned fixture and a draw. It would have been too late to get a programme produced in time for this game.

The first thing I noticed when I got into the stadium was that the pitch was frozen solid. It looked more like a lumpy ice rink and I wondered if they'd have been playing had there not been such a huge fixture backlog. Still, Chelsea had played their postponed match against Newcastle on the same surface forty-eight hours earlier and hammered the then-leaders 4–0 in a sublime display of attacking football. The *Express* reckoned it had been the brightest afternoon at Stamford Bridge since 'wayward stars like Peter Osgood and Alan Hudson were in their prime'.

I stopped off at the club shop before taking my seat and treated myself to a knitted hat and scarf set (£3.50, which I'd claim back on expenses). This wasn't because I had any affection for Chelsea, but because this was one of the coldest nights I'd ever known.

As the teams ran out, I took in all the familiar faces from my seat high up in the East Stand (£4.25, which I'd also claim back on expenses). Clive Walker was the undoubted individual star, but I also recognized Micky Droy, the massive centre-half, 'Chopper' Harris and Mike Fillery. The team's stylish passing game was their hallmark and they were spraying the ball around impressively as they warmed up.

I didn't recognize any of the Wigan players.

As the game got underway, it became apparent that several players had chosen the wrong footwear. It was especially notice-able that Chelsea's young central defence pairing of Kevin Hales and Colin Pate were having trouble staying on their feet. The Wigan right-back provided the first-half comedy highlight with a sliding tackle that kept on going, eventually taking him all of ten yards past Walker, who he was trying to dispossess.

Things weren't going entirely to plan for the home side. Everything Chelsea tried seemed a little overambitious, given the conditions, while Wigan were content to play a basic game. The goal rush I was there to witness looked like it wouldn't be materializing.

In the fortieth minute, Tommy Gore, Wigan's diminutive midfielder, sent a shockwave through the Stamford Bridge crowd when he gave his side an unexpected lead, darting in from nowhere to catch Petar Borota stranded on his six-yard line with a delicate chip into the top left-hand corner of the net. His teammates slid in from all around to congratulate him.

The second half was all Chelsea, but it was one of those nights. Veteran goalkeeper John Brown was in sublime form, despite his cartilage problems. One save from Walker was one I'll never forget. And on the few occasions Chelsea got past Brown, the woodwork came to his rescue.

When the final whistle went, the Wigan players went wild, and I couldn't help but feel happy for them. Their game plan of keeping things simple had worked. I had gone to Stamford Bridge expecting a scoreline in double figures and ended up seeing something even more exciting – the biggest Cup shock I had ever witnessed. In my mind this was vindication for sacrificing my Civil Service job for the romance of the Cup eight years earlier. That decision had led me to where I was now – the breath of fresh air that advertising so desperately needed.

Back at the hotel, after carefully packing the programmes into my overnight bag I helped myself to several whiskies from the minibar (the expenses were rapidly adding up) and watched *Zulu* on ITV. It was a shame Caroline wasn't with me. We'd hoped she could get time off work to make a long weekend of it, including watching Blondie at the Hammersmith Odeon, but the hospital were short-staffed because of the flu epidemic and she was needed there.

During the advert breaks I imagined my WASS commercial alongside the best of the current crop – the Discos ad with dancing crisps, the Aero ad which seemed to suggest that the chocolate bar was healthy because of the bubbles, and the attempts by the government to get people walking and thereby feeling less depressed. Obviously it wouldn't be in the same league, but I felt it wouldn't be out of place in such illustrious company.

The next day, I was relieved to see my newly appointed WASS spokesman waiting outside the studio. He was wearing a black suit that looked, on closer inspection, as though it had come straight from the racks of the Oxfam shop, right down to the frayed cuffs and stubborn stains. The glazed expression on his face and a strong smell of Polo mints led me to suspect that the George Best similarities didn't end with the way he looked and his accent.

But once the camera started rolling, he seemed fine to me, delivering a strong, confident performance, although I struggled to make out one or two of the words. The good thing was that he was different and would therefore stand out. I felt as though my decision had been thoroughly justified and was already looking forward to my next commercial, hopefully one with a bigger budget. It had all gone a lot more smoothly than I'd imagined. The director handed me a cassette without comment and I set off back to Leeds.

Whenever anyone made a TV commercial at the agency, the entire staff would gather together for a viewing. I was beaming with pride as I put the cassette into the video recorder and pressed Play. The next fifteen seconds were the worst of my life. At first there was a kind of stunned silence, followed by uproarious laughter. One person who wasn't amused was the chairman, who later described it as 'an embarrassment to the agency'.

When I watched it again, I could see his point. It wasn't the maverick, game-changing, daring piece of brilliance I'd previously imagined. In reality, it was a scruffy, bewildered-looking drunk who was more likely to frighten off potential customers than attract them, mumbling incoherently about used cars. The commercial appeared only half a dozen times, usually late at night when no one was watching. The client refused to pay for it.

That wasn't even the worst part. When I put in my expenses claim, almost all of it was declined. I was given the cost of the train fare, hotel and meals; I had to cover the rest, including the football ticket, programmes, hat and scarf, taxi to and from Stamford Bridge and minibar. Which meant I was around £25 out of pocket. On the plus side, I had a once-in-a-lifetime programme.

If there was one thing I learned from Wigan's upset win it was that you could go a long way just by doing the basics well, working hard and not trying anything too ambitious. I decided to apply that to my professional life and for the next few months I kept my head down and learned how to write ads. It seemed to do the trick. Although my career at the agency would forever be tainted by the WASS commercial, I at least managed to put together a decent portfolio, which was enough to get me a job with one of Manchester's better agencies.

Caroline and I moved across the Pennines that June, and a couple of months later I rented a suit that was a lot more impressive than my Irish presenter's for our wedding at a small church in Devon.

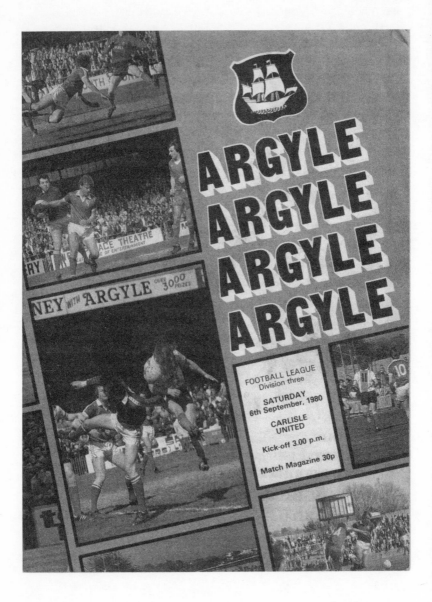

ARGYLE
ARGYLE
ARGYLE
ARGYLE

FOOTBALL LEAGUE
Division three

SATURDAY
6th September, 1980

CARLISLE
UNITED

Kick-off 3.00 p.m.

Match Magazine 30p

20

Plymouth Argyle v. Carlisle United,
6 September 1980

POST BOX. Another new feature in this season's 'Argyle'. A page where you can express your views. Moan! Groan! Congratulate! Opinionate! Let's be hearing from you. The address! 'Post Box', Argyle, Home Park, Plymouth (Editor).

From the official programme

We'd had a brilliant honeymoon driving around the West Country for a week, and Caroline had readily agreed to stop off at Home Park on the way back to Manchester. She even seemed to be quite excited about the prospect of seeing her first ever football match, despite the fact that it was Plymouth Argyle against Carlisle. Besides, we both relished the thought of getting away from the car for a few hours and the attention it attracted.

It was a Vauxhall Viva we'd owned for about a year, and it had been fine until the wedding, when one of the guests, who was fascinated with my new wife's chest, had sprayed THERE ARE TWO BIG REASONS I MARRIED CAROLINE on the rear window. This was quite amusing until we discovered that spray paint had been used, which had proved impossible to remove.

I was understandably nervous as we took our seats in the main stand, because this was one of the most crucial games of my life. If Caroline enjoyed it, it could mean a lifetime of going to football together and watching forty or more games a season, instead of wondering if I could sneak away to the odd match on my own or with Nick, my brother-in-law. I bitterly regretted the fact that it was a Third Division fixture. It would have been much easier to persuade her how brilliant football was if it involved someone like Liverpool or Nottingham Forest.

She was already feeling a bit let down, after my promised two-week honeymoon in Reykjavik had been downscaled, for financial reasons, to a somewhat less exotic week of Cornwall B&Bs, so I was desperate for her to enjoy herself. I was acutely aware that the last time I'd tried to share my love of the game with a woman (Mandy at Crystal Palace), it had backfired in a spectacular manner, so I needed to make sure I got it right this time.

I decided on a strategy of getting overly enthusiastic at every good piece of play or incident, hoping that this would be contagious. I started by describing my previous visit to Home Park (leaving out the bits about the dice), and telling her how she was going to love Fred Binney. In advertising terms, he was Plymouth's Unique Selling Proposition, so it made sense to build him up. Or at least it would have done had he been playing. When I looked out at the teams warming up, there was no sign of him. An impostor was wearing his number 9 shirt.

Enquiries revealed that my hero had gone to Hereford (which I now knew was in England) earlier in the year. The previous season's Player of the Year apparently hadn't fitted in with new manager Bobby Saxton's plans, which led me to believe that his plans must have been rubbish. This major scandal hadn't, for some reason, made the national papers. I had to hide my disappointment, despite feeling cheated by my hero's absence.

'Wasn't that great?' I remarked to Caroline as David Kemp, the man who now wore Fred Binney's shirt, kicked off. Perhaps raving about someone's ability to kick off a football match was a bit much, but I was feeling under immense pressure. I needed a spectacular game, with goals, sendings-off, controversy and excitement. This was a lot to expect from two teams with just one win between them. Still, I did have one incredible fact up my sleeve for when there was a dull patch in play.

It wasn't long before I was forced to produce it, as the opening minutes produced little in the way of entertainment.

'You know what's really interesting about this game?' I asked my wife.

As expected, this was met with a glum shake of the head.

'It's the league's longest away round trip. Nearly seven hundred and eighty miles.'

She didn't look quite as fascinated as I'd hoped, and I was grateful to the young Carlisle centre-forward for bringing the game to life. First, he played a stunning forty-yard pass to the unmarked winger George McVitie, who controlled it nicely before crossing. Then he turned quickly on a throw-in and his shot from outside the box missed the post by inches.

'Did you see *that*?' I said, a little too enthusiastically.

Next it was Chris Harrison's turn to get in on the action. The Argyle full-back ran straight at the defence and unleashed a shot from twenty-five yards out. Trevor Swinburne in the Carlisle goal got down, but couldn't hold on to the ball. David Kemp blasted it home from close range and the fans all around us leapt to their feet. 'What a great goal!' I shouted, possibly guilty of a slight exaggeration. I was definitely warming to Kemp, though. Maybe one day I'd be able to forgive him for taking Fred Binney's place.

A couple of minutes later, Carlisle equalized through left-winger Gordon Staniforth's brilliant (it really was) volley from a Houghton header. This was turning into a really exciting game and Caroline was starting to enjoy herself, even protesting when Forbes Phillipson-Masters was booked for kicking the ball away as the visitors prepared to take a free kick.

A minute after that she was even more vocal. The Carlisle centre-forward played a one-two with McVitie and raced clear through the middle before being chopped down from behind by Phillipson-Masters. Referee Mr Bung (according to the programme) or Mr Bune (according to that morning's paper) from Cranleigh, Surrey had no hesitation in producing a red card and Plymouth were down to ten men. I got out my just-acquired Plymouth Argyle souvenir pen and wrote 'SENT OFF (26 minutes)' next to Phillipson-Masters' name in the programme (or match magazine, as they called it). It was important to keep a proper record.

The Carlisle centre-forward, who looked about sixteen, was causing all sorts of problems, and Caroline asked me what his name was. I looked down the team list.

'Peter Beardsley,' I said. 'Not bad is he?'

The first half was drawing to a close when Plymouth's Donal Murphy went on a run down the left and put in a cross which was met on the volley by the increasingly brilliant David Kemp, to give Plymouth a deserved 2–1 lead. The fans behind the goal burst into song to the tune of 'Lily the Pink':

We'll drink a drink a drink to David the Kemp, the Kemp, the Kemp,
The saviour of the Plymouth forward line.
And so we gave him
A little white football,
And now he's scoring all the time.

These words provoked a brief feeling of bitterness at the injustice of our lyrically superior York City song failing to catch on like this one clearly had, but I soon got over it. Besides, I quite liked it.

It had been forty-five minutes of unexpectedly exhilarating football. I went off to get us both a cup of tea and a Cornish pasty (we'd been pretty much living on these for the past week) while Caroline read the programme. Or at least that was the idea. When I got back it was on my seat. Clearly unread. I hid the hurt I was feeling and asked if she was enjoying herself. I felt almost irrationally happy when she confirmed that she was.

There was only time to briefly flick through the programme before the game kicked off again, but it was enough time to register that the editor didn't appear to have fully understood the concept of a letters page (or 'Post Box', as he called it), since he seemed happy to print pretty much anything that arrived in the mail, such as the following from Mr P. M. Healey of Wiltshire:

Dear Sir,
Please continue to send me Argyle Lottery tickets on a weekly basis. I enclose £4, being for lottery nos. 154, 155, 156 and 157 at £1 each.
Yours faithfully,
P. M. Healey

And this from a fan in Littlehampton, Sussex:

Dear Sir,
I'm sending a 25p postal order to join the Supporter's Association. I've enclosed a s.a.e.
Yours sincerely,
Hazel Sargent

The rest of the programme would have to wait until we got home, as the outstanding David Kemp and his teammates were already back on the field, lining up in an innovative 3–3–3 formation. Caroline was definitely showing an interest in the game and actually seemed excited about the prospect of another forty-five minutes.

Plymouth showed no signs of being disadvantaged by being a man down, and relentlessly attacked the Carlisle goal. Of the opposition, only Peter Beardsley was looking as though he belonged at Third Division level. The rest of his team would have struggled to get a game with Bromley.

Then David the Kemp the Kemp the Kemp (I couldn't get the song out of my head) struck again to complete his hat-trick and simultaneously eradicate all memory of the unskinny Fred Binney. It was a crisp finish from another Murphy cross, and this time Caroline jumped up to join in the celebrations. It seemed I no longer needed to try to persuade her how good the game was. She was perfectly capable of seeing for herself.

It was left to Donal Murphy to finish off the scoring, when he ran on to a Brian Bason cross to thunder a header past the helpless Swinburne. A few minutes later, Bason was booked (a fact that I carefully noted in my programme), and just before the end Carlisle's Staniforth had a shot tipped on to the bar by Geoff Crudgington.

That was the last act of the game, for Mr Bune (or Bung) blew the final whistle. As if to confirm his supernatural aura, the setting sun picked out the blond highlights in David the Kemp the Kemp the Kemp's hair as he walked off to a standing ovation, having now scored five goals in the first four league games of the season.

Looking at the Carlisle fans trudging out of the ground, I wondered how I could call myself a proper football fan compared to these people. They would have had to have left their beds at around four o'clock on a freezing autumn morning just so they could make a sixteen-hour round trip to watch a useless team that had got one point and two goals all season. These were true fans. Either that or certifiably insane.

Caroline and I went back to the car, her coat tightly wrapped around the two big reasons why I married her. I asked her if she wanted to go to another game some time, and her reply warmed my heart: 'Only if it's to see Plymouth.'

I looked at the fixture list on the inside back page of the programme. She was in luck. We were planning on spending Christmas with her parents. And Argyle just happened to be playing their local rivals Exeter on Boxing Day.

Driving back meant putting up with blaring horns and flashing headlights, as people read the writing on the rear windscreen. We were used to it now, although Caroline never really got used to passing drivers craning their necks to try to get a look at her chest.

Back in Manchester, we managed to keep up on all the Argyle news with a brilliant new scheme set up by the club. You just rang Plymouth 509754 and got all the latest news from Home Park. Or, as they put it in the programme advert, 'How's Foster's Fibula? Bason's Bruises? Murphy's Spuds? Ring 509754.' And ring it I did, several times a week, usually from work. I didn't want a repeat of the Fred Binney scandal, when I was completely unaware of his having left the club.

A few weeks later we bought our first home, a small terraced house literally around the corner from the Gardeners in Chorlton. Location is everything when it comes to property, and this couldn't have been in a more perfect place. It was within walking distance of United's Old Trafford and a short bus ride from City's Maine Road.

CLARET

Burnley Football Club

BURNLEY v
PLYMOUTH ARGYLE
Football League Division Three, Saturday, 20th Dec. 1980. Volume 11 Match 16.

Official Match Programme 25p

21

Burnley v. Plymouth Argyle,
20 December 1980

Traditionally today is the worst day of the year for clubs to
attract spectators to their grounds.

From the official programme

We'd left Manchester early for the Burnley v. Plymouth Argyle
game as bad weather threatened to make the drive slow going.
On the plus side, the snow covered the THERE ARE TWO BIG
REASONS I MARRIED CAROLINE graffiti which was now a
permanent feature of the rear window. Another worrying
aspect, on top of the weather, was my doubts over the car's
ability to get there. I had a distinct feeling that the rattling and
thumping that had been coming from under the bonnet
recently might be a bad sign. I'd been so worried that earlier in
the week I'd joined AA Relay, just in case.

I wasn't really expecting the Viva to make it to Burnley, even
though it was only around thirty-five miles away, so I hadn't
allowed myself to get excited about the prospect of seeing
Plymouth Argyle again. But when we reached the outskirts of
the town and started seeing well-wrapped fans in claret and

blue making their way to the ground, the familiar feelings of anticipation started bubbling up inside me.

We got there with an hour to spare before kick-off. This was just as well since Caroline suddenly expressed an urgent need to find a newsagent, so we drove around until we found one. She dashed inside, came out with a paper and seemed to be stuffing something else under her coat. We then found a car park near the ground and made our way in, taking extra care not to slip on the icy pavements.

I had a soft spot for Burnley. They were in Division Three for the first time in their history and I remembered seeing them on *Match of the Day* the previous season (when they were relegated), losing 7–0 at QPR. Their young reserve goalkeeper Billy O'Rourke made his first-team debut that day and the cameras had caught him going off in tears afterwards. It was one of the saddest things I'd seen in football, and I was pleased to see that not only was he still with the club, he was having an exceptional season for the reserves, conceding a goal every two games or so.

You know it's not going to be your day when you scald your mouth biting into a pre-match pie, and that was exactly what happened to me. And that wasn't the only sign of impending doom. Caroline had picked up a copy of the *Burnley Express and Times* at the shop, and there was a small piece in it about how the home team gaffer, Brian Miller, was on a streak of incredible luck. Not only had he picked up £1,000 in last Saturday's weekly lottery, he'd also won a colour television in the club's Christmas draw. Things were not looking good for Plymouth.

The crowd was on the small side, but as the programme pointed out, that was the fault of the Football League for making them play on a day when everyone was doing their Christmas shopping. It was good for me and Caroline, though, as it meant we got really good seats.

As she sat down, her mind seemed to be elsewhere so I tried to get her interested in what we were about to watch, by quoting statistics from the programme. It was not a success.

Both sides were challenging for promotion, although Plymouth had recently gone off the boil. The game began with Burnley looking the more threatening and Billy Hamilton, the Northern Ireland international, tormenting the Plymouth defence. At least David the Kemp the Kemp the Kemp was looking his usual brilliant self. He was already on nineteen goals for the season, despite shockingly going on a streak of nine games without scoring. Presumably he had an injury he was keeping from everyone. I kept ringing the Plymouth hotline from work, desperately hoping manager Bobby Saxton wasn't going to drop him, and so far he'd kept his place.

The thirteenth minute was always a time for increased anxiety for me at a football match, because thirteen had been my unlucky number ever since I conceded as many when keeping goal for my Boy Scouts team. This is why I wasn't remotely surprised when Burnley opened the scoring after exactly thirteen minutes. From a corner, eighteen-year-old Vince Overson outjumped the defence to head the ball back across the goal, and top scorer Steve Taylor placed a nice header just inside the far post. Brian Laws nearly doubled the score a minute later, but his shot was brilliantly saved by Geoff Crudgington.

Moments later, David the Kemp the Kemp the Kemp had a shot blocked on the line, and then referee Trelford Mills (Barnsley), who had until then been frozen out of the action, went on a yellow card waving spree, booking Plymouth's George Foster for sulkily throwing the ball away, Forbes Phillipson-Masters for an innocuous foul, and Burnley's Laws for an overenthusiastic challenge on Murphy.

Things got worse for Plymouth just after the break, when

Taylor beat Crudgington from just inside the area to make it 2–0. If I'd been a fair and impartial observer, I would have said that the second goal was well deserved and that the scoreline was an accurate representation of the game so far, but to me it was an act of gross injustice.

But as anyone who knew anything about football realized, you didn't keep David the Kemp the Kemp the Kemp quiet for long. He made a brilliant run into the box before being chopped down and falling flamboyantly to the floor. Mr Mills pointed equally dramatically to the spot, and Donal Murphy pulled the score back to 2–1. Caroline, who had been a bit distracted the whole game, didn't even seem to notice. It was as though she had something else on her mind.

The game was end-to-end action and it was no surprise when David the Kemp the Kemp the Kemp's perfectly placed header eluded Stevenson in the Burnley goal to level the scores. I was so busy hugging Caroline in celebration that I failed to notice the referee had disallowed it for a push on a defender. It was thirteen minutes before full time.

That was the last time Plymouth looked like scoring, and Burnley could easily have made the margin bigger on the stroke of full time when Potts had a great shot tipped around the post by the impressive Crudgington.

We walked back to the car park, a little despondent. It had been a day when nothing had worked out, and it didn't get any better when Caroline told me to wait in the car as she'd suddenly realized that she'd forgotten something. I asked her if she wanted me to go with her, but she said it was fine. And then, for the second time since we'd arrived in Burnley, she went off to do something she wouldn't tell me about.

I was thankful that I had the programme to keep my mind occupied while she was gone, so I put the interior light on and eagerly started reading it.

The Puzzle Page had a unique way of ensuring that no one walked away with the prize of two tickets for any home league game. 'Today's puzzle competition should not be too difficult for you soccer fans to solve,' it announced. They were right. It wasn't difficult, it was impossible. Alongside a picture of Peter Mellor, the former Burnley goalkeeper I'd once seen at Highbury, were the words, 'Take a look at the photograph and let us know who the two former Burnley players are,' with the helpful addition, 'We'll give you a clue – both players have appeared at Wembley.' However hard I looked, I could only see one player.

I then had the luxury of being able to read through the list of ball sponsors for the entire season, study every advert in detail (my favourite was a cartoon cow dressed in a superhero outfit to advertise Super Beef from Peter Todd Meats Ltd) and even attempt the Clarets' Crossword with my newly acquired Burnley souvenir pen (I was stumped by the crucial 1 Across, which was 'Scoring the second most vital goal').

I wondered if Caroline would be interested in hanging around for a bit so we could see 'LYNNE ALLAN – Vivacious young female vocalist' who was appearing later at the Centre Spot social club in the Main Stand. This was a club that was famous throughout the north-west for attracting just three people for a televised England game, so I hoped Lynne Allan's expectations were low.

I'd been so engrossed in the programme I had no idea how long Caroline had been gone. It can't have been that long, but when she got back her eyes were gleaming with excitement. She made no attempt to explain why she'd kept me waiting in the freezing cold. It would be five more days before I found out.

The journey back was notable for being the last one we made in the Viva. Somewhere along the M65 the thumping sound from under the bonnet started getting worse, and I announced that I was stopping at the next AA phone box, adding, 'I reckon the big end's gone.' I didn't actually know what this was, but I'd been in a friend's car when a similar thing happened and that was what he'd said.

After finding an AA box by the side of the road, I rang and was told they'd be there within the hour. The snow was getting heavy and the temperature couldn't have been far from freezing. I kept the engine running so we could keep the heater on. While we were waiting, Caroline got so bored that she started reading the programme. It was at times like this that I was glad I always bought two. It meant we could have one each to study.

Less than an hour later, as promised, the AA tow truck pulled up and a man got out.

'What's the problem?' he asked, adjusting his peaked cap.

'There's a noise coming from the engine – he thinks the big end's gone,' Caroline replied, with a touching faith in my mechanical knowledge.

I felt my face reddening.

'Right,' said the AA man, opening the bonnet. 'Let's have a look, shall we?'

After poking around for a few minutes, he resurfaced with the news that the engine mounts were loose and we were unlikely to make it back to Chorlton. And this was when joining AA Relay suddenly paid off. The idea was that they towed the car either home or to the garage of your choice – and gave you a lift at the same time. It felt quite humiliating being dropped off outside the house by a tow truck, but luckily it was dark.

There was no point getting the Viva fixed. It was a rubbish car anyway, especially with the impossible-to-remove TWO BIG REASONS graffiti, and we managed to find someone who would tow it away and use it for parts. I'd already found a replacement: a friend of a friend was selling his Mini Van and I was assured that it was a really good deal. Fortunately, we'd done all our

Christmas shopping so we didn't need a car until Boxing Day, when we'd be driving down to Devon. This gave us the perfect excuse to spend the next few days at home, eating and watching TV, starting with a magnificent Saturday night double bill of *The Little and Large Show* followed by *Dallas*.

On Christmas morning, before opening our presents (I hoped mine was the full-size football game on metal legs from House of Holland that I'd been lusting after), we opened our cards. Most were for both of us, but two of the envelopes had my name on them and I recognized Caroline's writing on both. But only one was from her. I tore open the other one and pulled out a card that said 'Happy 9th Birthday' on the front, with '9th birthday' crossed out and 'Christmas' scribbled in its place. Inside it read:

The gayest birthday ['birthday' was crossed out and 'Christmas'
      written in] greetings,
   the best of wishes, too,
   for happiness and lots of luck
   in everything you do.

It then said 'Best wishes from Plymouth Argyle' and was signed by the entire team – John Sims, Forbes Phillipson-Masters, Kevin Hodges and the rest of the side currently sliding down the Third Division table. I stared at David the Kemp the Kemp the Kemp's signature (he only signed with one 'Kemp') a little longer than was strictly necessary. His handwriting was as flamboyant as his football.

The newsagent we'd stopped off at had apparently run out of Christmas cards, but Caroline hadn't let that stop her. As for the age discrepancy, apparently she was so embarrassed about getting the players to sign a card for a twenty-five-year-old that she'd had to invent a nine-year-old nephew.

As I stared at the card, that routine Third Division match-up between Burnley and Plymouth Argyle we'd seen a few days ago was suddenly elevated from instantly forgettable to one I'd always remember fondly. Even after the disappointment of a defeat that had put the club five points adrift of the leading three, every single one of the players had still managed to sign a Christmas card that had been passed around the Plymouth dressing room. Just for me.

I wondered if that would have happened with any of the bigger clubs.

Arranging to get it signed was one of the nicest, kindest, most thoughtful things anyone had ever done for me, and showed that there were a lot more than just two big reasons why I married Caroline.

REPLAY

Thursday 14th May 1981 Kick off 7.30pm

One-Hundredth Football Association Challenge Cup Competition

FINAL TIE

Manchester City v Tottenham Hotspur

Wembley Stadium

Official programme 60p

22

Manchester City v. Tottenham Hotspur, 14 May 1981

The days of the classic finals may never be seen again and the hope of high scoring between Tottenham Hotspur and Manchester City was easier to express than to fulfil.

From the official programme

I heard a weedy-sounding horn tooting outside and looked out of the window. It was my brother-in-law, Nick, waiting in his gold Fiesta 950. This particular model was mockingly known as a 'social worker's car' among my work colleagues, and it didn't help counter the stereotype that Nick was, in fact, a social worker.

Quickly finishing my lunch of Unger's Chipsteak, a tasteless, insipid (or 'mouthwateringly delicious' as I described it in the ads I wrote) beef product which I bought in bulk from our client, I grabbed my bomber jacket, rushed out of the door and climbed into the back seat. Nick, his brother David and I were going to Wembley for the Cup Final replay between Manchester City and Spurs.

The first game had taken place five days earlier and ended in a 1–1 draw. I'd watched it something like sixteen times, due to a combination of recently renting our first ever video recorder for £15.95 a month (and then extravagantly adding a remote control unit for a further £1.95 a month), and Caroline working nights. I'd tried the machine out by successfully recording the final on the Saturday. I was fascinated by the Philips VR2020's ability to play in grainy slow motion and I spent hours analysing parts of the match, like Tommy Hutchison's goal for City and his own goal for Spurs, trying to find things I'd missed at normal speed. It was like having an unlimited number of my very own action replays.

It could also record while you were out, a feature that would be fully tested tonight. Programming had been complex, especially as I wanted to include the *Top of the Pops Cup Final Special* which was on beforehand. But after several test runs I was confident that it would work. The brilliant bit about this was that I would watch the game live at Wembley and then come home and watch it again at around three in the morning, a couple of hours before Caroline got home. I was particularly excited about seeing Spurs, who seemed impossibly glamorous, having signed not one but two foreign players, Ossie Ardiles and Ricky Villa, both from Argentina.

The drive down the M1 felt like being part of a massive procession to Wembley: just about every car, lorry and coach had pale blue scarves either flying from their windows or draped across the back seat. Nick had made a compilation tape for the trip which was made up of football-themed songs. Inevitably, 'Ossie's Dream' was one of these, a slightly awkward Chas and Dave cash-in notable for rhyming 'Wembley' with 'trembly'. The only controversial song choice was the inclusion of Altered Images' 'Dead Pop Stars', which had a slightly tenuous link to the theme: their singer, Clare Grogan, had been in the film *Gregory's Girl*, which was sort of about football. I couldn't wait for it to come out on video as I'd already seen it three times at the pictures.

The journey wasn't entirely free of drama. Just before Northampton, a van hit us from behind, pushing us into the car in front. Since we were all on the way to the Cup Final, details were exchanged in record time before everyone got on with the journey, even though the front of the Fiesta was smashed up and the headlights were pointing in opposite directions.

When we finally limped into London, Nick parked outside his mate's house in Wembley Park Drive and we walked the short distance to the ground. Wembley Way was packed and movement was slow. Suddenly, I felt a hefty blow to my bum, as someone's boot made solid contact. I looked around, but everyone was staring straight ahead, lost in their own little worlds. My first ever experience on the receiving end of football hooliganism was a complete anticlimax. Someone had kicked me in the bum and then either run away or cleverly blended in with the crowd. My assailant had got away with possibly the most rubbish assault ever committed in the vicinity of a football ground and I had no idea why he (or she) had done it.

As we arrived at Entrance 29, I handed Nick and David their tickets. I'd taken Monday morning off to queue for them at City's Maine Road ground, but when I'd arrived, the place was virtually deserted. I had been expecting half the population of Manchester to be there, with queues stretching for miles. Instead I was faced with a couple of dozen diehards, one of whom had obviously been thinking along similar lines as he had brought along a collapsible chair and was clutching a Thermos flask and sandwiches.

The tickets had cost £10 each, a sum so high that my hand shook as I wrote out the cheque. I couldn't believe how easy it had been to get them and suspiciously held one up to the light, to make sure it was real. The lion's head watermark confirmed that it was, and we got into the stadium without any problems.

We found our seats, which were in the South Stand, giving us a really good view of both goals. It was slightly sore sitting down and I could have done with a cushion, but other than that, conditions were perfect. It was a fairly warm, still spring evening, around sixteen degrees, and the ground was filling quickly. Several Argentinian flags only added to the atmosphere, as did the chanting of 'There's only one Tommy Hutchison' from both sets of fans. Nick had to explain to his confused-looking brother that this was because Hutchison had scored for both teams in the first game.

Inevitably, a marching band then appeared, which was my cue to take a good look at the programme, which I'd got on the way in. I was impressed with how quickly they'd managed to produce it. There was a full report on Saturday's game and much was made of this being the hundredth FA Cup Final.

As I looked at the City team photo, I thought of them in their changing room. I knew exactly what would be happening as I'd seen a Granada documentary a few months back which took viewers behind the scenes when John Bond replaced Malcolm Allison as manager. It had footage of the pre-match team talks. He swore a lot less than Allison, which I found pleasing, and would be telling each player what was expected of them. Most would be listening intently, although on the televised talk the curly-haired number 4 seemed more keen on checking his hair in the mirror than listening to his gaffer.

I glanced at my watch, which Caroline had bought for me with her tax rebate. It was 6.55. Right now, in a terraced house hundreds of miles away, a Philips VR2020 would be switching itself on while Tommy Vance was introducing *Top of the Pops* on BBC1. It was like something out of *Tomorrow's World*. I was in awe of technology.

I kept glancing up from the programme, expecting to see the

marching band marching off, but they had arranged themselves in a U formation by the tunnel and were standing still. For a moment I was gripped by a fear that they were staging some kind of pitch occupation, but relaxed when I saw the obscure Royal Family member who they'd managed to get at short notice walking down the red carpet to be presented to the teams.

In real life you can't fast forward through this kind of thing, but once I got home I'd have the luxury of pressing a button and watching it whizz by in seconds. I loved my video recorder.

David was a lifelong City fan, and Nick and I had decided to support them as well. We didn't have much choice, given that we were in a part of the ground that held around thirty thousand of them. A huge cheer went up every time a City player waved in our direction and it was easy to feel part of the team, even if it was only temporary. To help us pass the time, we held a competition for who could spot the worst banner. Nick won easily by pointing out one that read RANSON WILL BE GALVINIZED, referring to City's full-back and future multi-millionaire Ray Ranson and Tottenham's winger with a degree in Russian studies, Tony Galvin.

I looked over at the Spurs players, picking out two in particular. Ricky Villa looked a lot chirpier than he had on Saturday, when he'd trudged off the pitch, dejected, after being substituted. I'd watched it several times in slow motion on video and he was definitely unhappy. But now he was chewing gum and smiling. Ossie Ardiles looked glum and serious, but then again, he always did.

By the time the game kicked off, the whole pitch apart from Joe Corrigan's goal was completely covered in a shadow, and the atmosphere was incredibly exciting. It only took about five minutes for the game to burst into life, when Steve Archibald's shot from a few yards out was smothered by Corrigan and rebounded to Ricky Villa – who else? – to score from close range. I was looking forward to seeing it again, as I had a suspicion that Tommy Caton (who had interrupted his A Level studies to play) had inadvertently set the goal up. This was something I'd be able to analyse when I got home.

The City supporters around us didn't lose heart. It was as though they knew their team weren't out of it yet. And only a few minutes later, before the excitement of the opening goal had had a chance to subside, they were level. Tommy Hutchison headed across for Steve MacKenzie to volley a beauty from twenty yards out. I don't think I'd ever felt such excitement at a match not involving Bromley. There had already been as many goals in the opening ten minutes as there had been in the entire first match, not to mention several near misses, great saves and even a shot cleared off the line. When Glenn Hoddle's near-perfect free kick hit the post a minute after the goal, Nick commented that this felt more like watching highlights than a full game.

Graham Roberts, who'd lost two teeth on Saturday, continued his run of bad luck by conceding a penalty when he pulled down Dave Bennett in the area. Kevin Reeves placed his kick into the right-hand corner and the City fans burst into a joyful rendition of 'Blue Moon'.

Spurs did not take this well, and this led to a spate of bookings: Ranson, Galvin, Archibald and Gerry Gow, a player who was twenty-eight according to the programme but looked at least forty, were all shown Mr Hackett's yellow card in the space of eight minutes. You could always tell when someone was in trouble with him. He'd make a fist, put his palm upward and then extend his index finger, bending it several times towards himself, as in 'come here'. Then he'd do the exact opposite – fist, palm downwards, index finger flicking rapidly – for 'go away'.

With discipline restored, Spurs pushed forward. And with twenty minutes left, Archibald controlled a Hoddle chip and was just about to shoot when Garth Crooks stole in to poke the ball home to level the scores. After this, both sides pressed hard for the winner as we drifted towards extra time.

By now, many of the City fans had left their seats and were standing. This meant that our view of Corrigan's goal was blocked. Which is how I managed to miss one of the greatest goals ever seen at Wembley.

What I saw was this. Garth Crooks got the ball on the edge of the area and passed to someone. Crooks then stood and watched as something clearly special unfolded. The excited screams coming from the Tottenham end grew louder and louder before exploding in a huge roar. All around me, heads dropped and mouths gawped in disbelief.

Spurs had scored. This was confirmed seconds later on the new giant electronic scoreboard, which read SPURS 3 MAN. CITY 2.

John Bond had said before the game that he'd rather lose a high-scoring thriller than win a boring one-niller. He got his wish. The whistle blew and the Cup was staying in London. Glenn Hoddle looked to be in tears, so I hated to think how the City players must have been feeling.

It took us five hours to get home, and for just about every minute of that time I was thinking of the video recorder, hoping I'd programmed it properly. We'd heard all about the Spurs winner on Nick's car radio. Apparently Ricky Villa had dribbled past four defenders (including Caton twice) for a truly wonderful individual goal. I couldn't wait to see it.

When we finally reached Chorlton, it was three a.m. As the adrenalin was still flowing, I grilled myself a Chipsteak, smothered it in brown sauce and took it through to the living room. After settling into the nearest armchair to the TV (the cord on the remote control didn't quite reach the couch), I rewound the tape to the beginning, pressed Play – and saw Una Stubbs acting out a charade for her teammates to guess. This was probably the first time in my life I hadn't been happy to see her, one of my biggest crushes, as it meant I'd somehow recorded ITV instead of BBC1. It seemed I was destined never to see Ricky Villa's goal.

I fast forwarded through the rest of *Give Us a Clue*, so depressed that I wasn't even amused by the sight of Lionel Blair's manic flailing arms during a speeded-up charade. I kept the button pressed down just to see what was on next, and I couldn't believe my eyes when I saw Wembley's twin towers and the caption CUP FINAL REPLAY. Apparently it had also been shown on ITV.

It felt hugely satisfying to speed through the pre-match formalities and get to the game itself. Jack Charlton, who was alongside Brian Moore, gave his expert opinion that Spurs would win and that Ricky Villa was due to have a good game. He ruined his credibility slightly by pronouncing the Argentinian's name as though it came after 'Aston'.

The game was just as exciting second time around. Caton had indeed accidentally set up the Spurs opener. MacKenzie's volley was perfect. But it was Villa's winner that would always stay in my memory, even though I'd technically missed it. A wonderful, graceful piece of brilliance. I must have watched it twenty times and was watching it in slow motion yet again when Caroline arrived home after her hospital shift.

'Look at this – you're not going to believe it!' I said excitedly, rewinding to the start of the move.

Caroline looked as impressed as you'd expect from someone who didn't really like football and had spent the last twelve hours on her feet working. 'Isn't it time you went to bed?' she said, without even acknowledging the Argentinian's brilliance. 'You have to get up again in a couple of hours.'

Going to the office was not a prospect that filled me with joy, especially after such a thrilling trip to London. I was getting a bit depressed by my inability to do even half-decent work since we'd crossed the Pennines. All I'd managed was a string of mildly embarrassing commercials in my first few months.

But there was one high-profile man in Manchester with far bigger problems.

UNITED REVIEW

MANCHESTER UNITED FOOTBALL CLUB

FOOTBALL LEAGUE
DIVISION ONE

United
v
**Wolverhampton
Wanderers**

Kick-off 3.00 p.m.

Saturday
3rd October 1981

25p

Volume 43, No. 5

1981-82 SEASON

OFFICIAL **PROGRAMME**

ARSENAL v UNITED, 26th SEPTEMBER 1981. Frank Stapleton came closer than anyone to breaking the deadlock at Highbury last Saturday when his best effort of the afternoon grazed the upright.

23

Manchester United v. Wolverhampton Wanderers, 3 October 1981

Garry made his first team debut two days after signing, in an away match versus Stoke City. Married to Sandra, the couple live in Wilmslow.

From the official programme

I felt a close bond with Garry Birtles. We'd both come to Manchester with glowing reputations, and both failed spectacularly to live up to them. His failings were slightly more visible than mine. In the twelve months since leaving Nottingham Forest for Old Trafford he'd managed two goals in thirty-odd games, which for a £1.25 million England striker with a European Cup winner's medal was considered disappointing. To seal our link, we were probably the only two men in the city still wearing full beards. Mine was there to cover up an awkward spot on my chin that stubbornly refused to go away; he'd grown his to be different. Apparently when he told this to Brian Clough, his previous gaffer, Clough had replied that if he wanted to do something different he should try scoring a few goals that Saturday.

I think what appealed to me most about Garry Birtles was the fact that he didn't just run away and hide, which is probably what I would have done. He'd been booed by his own supporters, laughed at by opposing ones, and had been described in a match report as playing such a small part in the game that he was 'bordering on the statuesque'. Despite this, I sensed that he was on the verge of coming good. In fact, we'd both shown signs of improvement in recent weeks: he'd managed finally to get his name on the scoresheet and I'd written a couple of ads that weren't totally embarrassing.

I was pleased to see that Ron Atkinson, who had replaced Dave Sexton at Old Trafford, hadn't dropped Birtles. Instead he'd signed Frank Stapleton from Arsenal in the belief that they'd form a deadly partnership. Much to the surprise of many football experts, this was starting to work.

As Caroline and I approached Old Trafford for the game with Wolves, we were both feeling good. One of the directors at work, Win, had arranged for us both to get season tickets (even though there was a long waiting list), which we had to pick up at the office. We went in and got them, full of excitement, before stopping off at the Supporters Club office to pick up my box of 'Treble Chance Lottery' 20p scratchcards, which I'd volunteered to sell to raise money. It was the least I could do after they had been kind enough to sort out the season tickets. There were a hundred Treble Chance cards in the box and I was confident of getting them all sold at work, which would raise £20 for the club. I tucked the box under my arm and followed the directions to the seat that would be mine for the next eight months.

It was one of those days when everything was going right. A beautiful autumn day, newly acquired Manchester United season tickets and a chance to share every game with my wife of little more than a year. Perhaps getting a little carried away by the euphoric mood, I scratched a couple of the cards – and immediately found myself 25p richer, with three matching symbols. The words WIN UP TO £1,000 INSTANTLY loomed large and I saw this as a sign that I should continue. Over the next twenty minutes I took part in a card-scratching frenzy that resulted in a small mountain of losing cards under my seat and a solitary 25p winner in my jacket pocket.

It was then that I noticed something. Caroline wasn't sitting next to me, unless she'd suddenly transformed into either a middle-aged man with a red and white bobble hat or a scrawny boy with an unconvincing moustache. I looked around frantically and finally saw her sitting about twenty yards away, a thunderous expression on her face. This was when I realized the importance of stressing that the seats should be together when you order two season tickets. I avoided eye contact with her after that, convincing myself that she might see the funny side of it by the time we got together after the match.

I became engrossed in the programme, hoping that if I studied it for long enough she'd calm down sufficiently to lose interest in glaring at me. Luckily, United's programmes were always packed with interesting stuff and I was soon immersed in a debate about whether all-seater stadiums would ever happen. Mr Gerard Noonan of Burnage had written in with his opinion, which was that the proposed £6 admission would be the last nail in the coffin for football in its present state, putting it out of reach for the average supporter. He seemed to have a point.

The programme also demonstrated that I wasn't the only one to sense a change in Garry Birtles' fortunes. The entire centre spread had been given over to him and was dominated by a picture of him sitting on the bonnet of a car that I hoped was his, holding the ball with which he'd scored against Swansea City. You were usually given a match ball after scoring a hat-trick, but in his case the criteria had apparently been down-graded. When you're Garry Birtles, it seemed, scoring once was considered an achievement. He was also featured on page two, playing a prank on the photographer by pulling the shirt over his face. This prompted the caption writer to claim that 'Birtles is the joker in the Old Trafford pack'. For good measure, another page featured a frame-by-frame breakdown of the other goal he'd scored in the past year, against Middlesbrough. Garry Birtles was clearly the man of the moment, and I had a feeling that Wolves were going to suffer.

It certainly wasn't looking like Sammy McIlroy's day. Before the match, a table was ceremoniously carried out on to the pitch and, in a typically flamboyant piece of showmanship, the United manager Ron Atkinson signed Bryan Robson in front of the forty-seven thousand spectators. Robson was now the most expensive player in British football and his signing almost certainly spelled the end for McIlroy, the last of the famous 'Busby Babes' and a real fan favourite. The problem with McIlroy was that while he created plenty, he simply didn't score enough goals.

Only a couple of points separated the teams, and on paper it looked like being a close one. Wolves had Andy Gray, who, until Robson's pre-match signing, had held the record for the highest transfer fee at just under £1.5 million. According to the ground announcer, Robson had signed with the same pen used by Gray. 'You'd think he could afford a new one,' mumbled my bobble-hatted neighbour grumpily.

From the moment the game kicked off, it was obvious that United were in a different class. Perhaps it was Robson's impending arrival that stirred some of the incumbents into action. McIlroy in particular was looking like the McIlroy of old, and when he put Stapleton through to score after less than ten minutes it felt as though the afternoon was going to provide something special.

Ten minutes later, McIlroy's day got even better. He picked up a weak clearance from Peter Daniel, a defender the programme astutely pointed out was 'of more value in a midfield role', and scored a rare goal with his left foot. I glanced over at Bryan Robson, who was sitting alongside his new gaffer, but he looked more happy than worried.

A few minutes later, Steve Coppell was brought down by George Berry on the edge of the area following a run through the middle. The fact that he was offside didn't seem to bother the referee, Mr Bridges of Deeside, who ignored his linesman and gave the free kick United's way. After persuading Ray Wilkins to stand aside, Sammy McIlroy curled a beautiful shot over the Wolves wall and into the top corner for his second and United's third.

If Robson was getting anxious, he was hiding it well. But even he must have felt a twinge of insecurity over what happened next.

Garry Birtles, who was having a superb game, passed to McIlroy, who ran at Joe Gallagher, the Wolves centre-half, before weaving inside and letting fly from twenty-five yards. Paul Bradshaw in the Wolves goal barely had time to raise a hand as he watched the ball whizz past him at astonishing speed. It was the best goal seen at Old Trafford all season. The roar of applause from the Stretford End was almost frighteningly loud, and all around me people stood up to join in. Sammy McIlroy, who was being replaced for not scoring enough goals, had got the first hat-trick of his career and was having his best ever game in a United shirt. He might have known his time was up, but he seemed determined to go out in a blaze of glory.

The perfect end to the perfect-day-apart-from-the-season-ticket-and-lottery-cards-debacles came when Stapleton played a Liam Bradyesque ball into the path of Birtles, who finished with such style and assurance that I and the other forty-seven thousand in the stadium instantly forgot how rubbish he'd been for the last year. The rarely heard chant of 'Birtles, Birtles!' echoed around Old Trafford, and I finally looked over in Caroline's direction, to see her smiling and clapping enthusiastically. Perhaps all was not lost.

The final score was 5–0, and it was the best I'd ever seen United play. McIlroy and Birtles, the two players most under pressure, had never been better. McIlroy got the match ball for the more traditional reason of getting a hat-trick; Bryan Robson had signed it 'To Sammy, from the most expensive sub in the game'. But it was Birtles, strangely, whose performance had made me happier. He finally looked at home in the United shirt and was visibly growing in confidence.

I waited for Caroline at the bottom of the stairs and soon realized that she was still unimpressed with the seating arrangements. I quickly agreed to see if I'd be able to exchange the ones we'd been allocated for some that were side by side. It didn't seem the right time to admit to losing nearly twenty quid on Treble Chance Lottery cards, so I decided to concentrate on positives instead and told her that I'd won 25p. She pointed out that since the ticket cost 20p in the first place I had, in fact, only won five pence.

When I went into work the following Monday, something had changed. Where I'd previously struggled over a blank sheet of paper, words suddenly started flowing and I managed to write three fairly good ads in the space of a day – something I hadn't done in the previous two months put together. I was particularly proud of one for Mamade, an instant marmalade mixture. It was as if some of Garry Birtles' newfound self-belief had rubbed off on me.

Over a curry that night I tried to convince Caroline that Birtles and I were cosmically linked, our fates inexorably bound together (I was listening to a lot of Kate Bush at the time). She thought that we had just taken our time settling into new jobs, and there was nothing mystical about it. I preferred my explanation.

When I told her that I'd had no luck exchanging the season tickets, she genuinely didn't seem to mind. With my slightly improved understanding of women, I realized that her interest was probably less in Manchester United and more in doing something together. After discussing several options, including taking up lawn bowls and learning to play the saxophone, we settled on badminton once a week, followed by a meal at the Azad Manzil in Chorlton, our favourite restaurant.

This felt like a good time to make the confession about my Treble Chance Lottery frenzy. She didn't seem impressed and vetoed my brilliant idea of getting another box and trying to win back the money I'd lost. Instead, I agreed to drive down to Old Trafford and hand over a cheque for £19.75 to Manchester United. The money I'd put aside for rent would probably now be going towards Bryan Robson's next perm.

When the spot on my chin finally disappeared a fortnight later, I decided to keep the beard. If it was good enough for Garry Birtles, it was good enough for me. For the next few months my professional ups and downs continued to mirror those of the former carpet fitter from Long Eaton. We even left Manchester at the same time nearly a year later, having finished work on the same day, which was an incredible coincidence.

Or at least Caroline thought it was. I knew different.

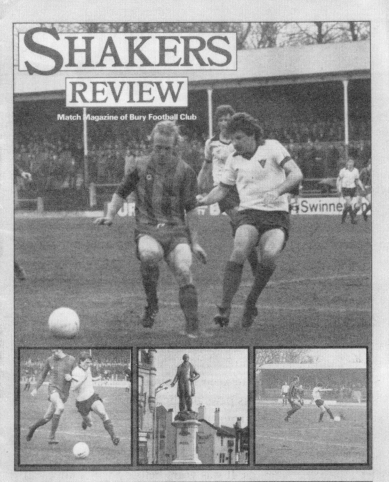

SHAKERS
REVIEW
Match Magazine of Bury Football Club

BURY v WIGAN ATHLETIC
At Gigg Lane, Bury
FOOTBALL LEAGUE DIVISION FOUR
Tuesday, 20th October 1981. Kick off 7.30 p.m.

Volume 82   **30p**   No. 7

24

Bury v. Wigan Athletic, 20 October 1981

The fact that Craig Madden has already reached a double figure goal tally shows the rewards which both the team and individuals can earn through putting extra work into their game.

From the official programme

When Caroline had to go away to a family reunion in the US for three weeks, I felt lost. It was the first time we'd been apart since getting married, and all I had for company at home was Sid the cat, who tried to keep me amused by standing on his hind legs and resting his paws on the remote control cord that stretched between my armchair and the TV.

Sid was the first cat I'd owned since losing Pigdog, whose habit of chasing cars and flinging himself at them had had its inevitable consequences. It was years before I felt ready to take on another one. But as fond as I was of Sid, and much as I was enjoying his performance, I felt I needed more in the way of stimulation. So when my friend Kevin's girlfriend was called away on business at the same time, it was as though the football gods were sending us a message. And the message was to cram as many matches into twenty-one days as possible.

Once we realized this, we got our fixture lists and Filofaxes out to plan an itinerary, coming up with an impressive fourteen matches, including nine in the first fortnight (or ten if you included a visit to the cinema for the film *Escape to Victory*, in which the Allied prisoners of war played the Germans at football). After a sensible start (Man Utd v. Birmingham), our travels took us to Stockport County v. Bradford City (where the programme tantalizingly hinted at a future 'programme swop' feature) before we found ourselves heading to Gigg Lane for our third game in four days, the local-ish derby between Bury and Wigan Athletic. And the main reason for our excitement was Craig Madden.

Madden looked more like the guitarist in a Scottish indie band than a footballer, but you couldn't pick up a newspaper without seeing his face or finding out about his latest goal-scoring exploits – as long as you were reading either the *Bury Times* or *Manchester Evening News*, that is. His fame now seemed on the verge of spreading nationwide as his two goals on Saturday had made him the league's leading marksman with twelve.

Showing a spectacular misjudgement of the fixture's appeal, we arrived a couple of minutes before kick-off, expecting to be able to park right outside the ground. This was a Tuesday night Fourth Division game, so the sight of vast swarms of people milling around the entrance trying to get in came as a shock. Perhaps the Craig Madden phenomenon was gathering momentum. More likely was the fact that this was the meeting of a team with a 100 per cent home record against local rivals who were unbeaten in their last nine games.

When we finally got through the turnstile we decided to sit down as we'd been doing a lot of standing in recent days. There was a man in a white coat standing at the entrance to a small section of wooden seats. We handed over the money and he gave us each a small ticket the size of a business card that had nothing but the words RESERVED CHAIR printed on it. We found seats (or should that be chairs?) behind a man in an expensive-looking sheepskin coat, who was sitting on his own.

As Kevin was as fascinated with programmes as I was, conversation was suspended until we'd both had a chance to read through it. As was our ritual for lower-division games, we scanned through the team lists, looking for familiar names. I found two, one on each side.

In both of the previous two years, Larry Lloyd had won European Cup medals with Nottingham Forest. This year, presumably bored with the monotony of it all, he'd decided to move to a mid-table Fourth Division side, Wigan, as player/manager. The other name I knew was, confusingly, playing for Wigan when I'd last seen him but was now wearing the number 4 shirt for Bury: Tommy Gore, scorer of that winning goal at Chelsea and inspirer of the GORE BLIMEY headline in the *Daily Express* the following day.

But Kevin seemed more excited by the sheepskin-clad man in front, elbowing me in the ribs and pointing at him. As I could only see the back of his head I had no idea who it was.

'It's only Peter Adamson,' Kevin whispered.

I made an impressed face and mouthed an 'awesome', then got back to my programme, unwilling to admit to not recognizing the name.

It's often the games you expect the least from that turn out to be the ones that deliver the most. And Bury against Wigan was easily the best of the fourteen we saw in those three weeks. One of the key ingredients of a really exciting local derby is a really rubbish referee. This ensures passion, controversy, furious protests from the players and a game that threatens to break out into open warfare. Thankfully, Mr Arnold Challinor of Rotherham was terrible. I'd seen him a few times, and the only thing that had stuck in my mind was that he seemed to run backwards a lot more than the average referee.

The first twenty minutes gave little indication of things to come – a cautious start by both sides, with only a couple of half chances. But then came the first signs that we were in for an outstanding evening. Bury full-back Dave Constantine whipped in a lovely cross and Mick Butler blatantly pulled down the ball with his arm before lashing it into the net, more out of frustration at his actions than anything else. Astonishingly, Mr Challinor pointed to the centre spot. The Wigan players surrounded him, demanding an explanation. Houghton was booked, followed a few minutes later by Larry Lloyd, whose inventive stream of abuse could be clearly heard where we were sitting. The visiting fans, who were opposite us, were throwing things on to the pitch. Then, with the match barely under control, there were further bookings for Paul Hilton after an X-rated tackle and Steve Johnson, who seemed to do nothing wrong but was shown a yellow card at the insistence of Larry Lloyd.

This was brilliant.

Having briefly managed to appease the Wigan player/gaffer, Mr Challinor then undid all his good work with another bizarre decision that went against the visitors. Graham Barrow had a header blocked on the line, but Houghton smacked in the rebound for the equalizer. Or at least it would have been had the referee not disallowed it for a non-existent handball. He wisely trotted away backwards in the opposite direction from where a fuming Larry Lloyd was standing.

At least the decisions didn't all go Bury's way. When Wigan finally got their equalizer, it was another goal that should never have been allowed. Mark Hilton was absolutely flattened, but play was predictably waved on and the move resulted in Bradd squeezing the ball home from a narrow angle.

As the first half ended, with the linesmen bravely escorting Mr Challinor from the pitch, someone behind me shouted in my direction, 'Oi, Len, does Rita know you're here?'

Was he talking to me? Did he think my name was Len? That made no sense. Not until the man in the sheepskin coat turned round and my heart almost exploded with excitement. It was Len Fairclough, Rita's husband from *Coronation Street*! He was currently part of a gripping storyline involving the building of a house, and I'd set the video to record the entire week's episodes using the special eight-hour cassette I'd bought for the Royal Wedding ('it will leave the others waiting at the church' boasted the magazine ad). I couldn't help noticing that he looked much smaller in the flesh.

In the programme's 'Half Time Teaser' quiz I only got one out of six (I knew that Jimmy Nicholson was Huddersfield's most capped player), but Kevin somehow got three (what kind of person would know that both league games between Wrexham and Lincoln in 1976/77 had exactly the same attendance?).

As we settled down for the second half, the ground was still buzzing with the incidents that had taken place in the opening forty-five minutes. But the crowd, officially given as 6,249, was about to have plenty more to talk about as Craig Madden took centre stage. Wigan defender Colin Methven's inept back pass was too weak to reach his keeper, who dashed out into a head-on collision with Madden, who got a boot to the ball, which trickled over the line.

Two minutes later, Mr Challinor, who had managed to stay out of the spotlight for a full seven minutes, strode back into it. He awarded Wigan a penalty when Hilton floored Wignall in full flight. The Shakers surrounded the official, protesting furiously, and he was apparently swayed by their arguments and changed his mind, awarding a free kick on the edge of the area instead. All eyes immediately sought out Larry Lloyd, but he just looked demoralized, his shoulders slumped as though the fight had gone out of him. His teammates weren't so accepting of their fate, and McMahon and Howard became the fifth and sixth names to go into Mr Challinor's book.

Graham Barrow became the next non-Bury player to help Bury's cause, by heading the ball straight to the feet of Craig Madden, the one player Wigan didn't want to see twelve yards out with just Bob Ward to beat. He did what everyone in the ground knew he would do and Bury were 3–1 up. This became 4–1 a few minutes later when Paul Hilton hit a curling left-foot strike from twenty-five yards out for the night's best goal.

This was enough for Larry Lloyd, who invoked his player/gaffer privileges and hauled himself off, but Wigan's luck didn't improve. Their left-back Jimmy Weston deflected a harmless cross beyond the stranded Ward and it was 5–1. Lloyd must have been praying that Manchester United would offer him a contract to cover for the injured Gordon McQueen, as had been rumoured in the press.

On the field, the drama continued right up to the end, the final minute producing two goals for the visitors through Barrow and Methven. It finished 5–3, with the bizarre sight of both sets of players surrounding the referee, who was trying to run off the pitch backwards. According to the programme, Mr Challinor was interested in gardening, badminton and table tennis. I suspected he'd have a lot more time to devote to these activities after this performance.

As we left our reserved chairs, my thoughts had already turned to the next night, a Wednesday, when we would be at Old Trafford for United against Middlesbrough. Thursday evening had been set aside for *Escape to Victory*, with a return to Edgeley Park for Stockport Reserves against Carlisle Reserves pencilled in for the Friday night. On Saturday we'd be at Maine Road for the clash between Manchester City and Forest.

The following week would be just as hectic, featuring another three games in four days: Stoke against Manchester City, Stockport and Mansfield, plus another visit to Gigg Lane for Craig Madden against Northampton. Kevin wanted to add a Hull game to the list, but I was a bit worried that I'd start looking as though I was obsessed, so I talked him out of it.

A fortnight later, I saw a copy of the *Wigan Reporter* that had been sent to the agency I worked for. This was commonplace: when we had ads in papers, we were sent 'voucher copies' as proof they had appeared and were printed properly. I turned to the back page and saw an article headed HEARTBREAK! DIARY OF DISASTER FOR THE LLOYD MEN. It was about the Bury game and contained an interview with the Wigan player/manager. When asked about the referee, Lloyd declared, 'If I said what I felt I'd be banned sine die. Their first goal was definitely a handball, our disallowed goal as good as any scored.' I don't know which impressed me more, his restraint or his casual use of a Latin phrase in the *Wigan Reporter*.

The *Bury Times* saw it differently, wisely preferring to concentrate on the undoubted genius of Craig Madden. Since that game we'd seen him get a breathtakingly brilliant hat-trick against Northampton. Kevin and I had become besotted, and this had forced us into a radical change of plan. Instead of a planned one-night break from football, we decided to go to Blackpool to see our third Bury game in a fortnight and witness our newfound hero consolidate the top scorer spot and pull even further away from Sheffield United's Keith Edwards.

If he could get just two goals in this game, he'd break the Fourth Division record for fastest to twenty in a season. And as if witnessing that wasn't an exciting enough prospect, there was also the fact that I was on the verge of getting my hands on something I had dreamt about since my early teens.

And it would happen before I even entered Blackpool's ground.

Blackpool
Football Club
Official Match Magazine

LEAGUE
DIVISION FOUR

Wednesday, 4th November, 1981
BURY
Kick-off 7.30 p.m.

PRICE
30p

25

Blackpool v. Bury,
4 November 1981

Fans have been saying that we'll have to watch Madden and Johnson as they've been getting among the goals. But I don't think we should concern ourselves with worrying about Bury . . . we'll let them worry about our players who are capable of scoring – and we've got more of them!

From the official programme

Although reaching most of life's important milestones had proved to be an anticlimax, I knew with absolute certainty that this one was going to be different. And that was why I was struggling to dampen the excitement that was preventing me from dropping off to sleep as I contemplated the Fourth Division game between Blackpool and Bury which was now less than twenty-four hours away.

How could I possibly relax, knowing that my one thousandth programme was just a short trip away up the M55? All I could think about was finally holding the landmark programme. In my mind, it would have a tangerine cover, perhaps with a picture of Stanley Matthews, their most famous player, and an article inside about Craig Madden, who was known (to me) as the Bury Stanley Matthews. It was surely no coincidence that both wore the number 7 shirt.

I'd spent much of the evening checking and double-checking, but each count yielded the same result. I had 999 different programmes. I was about to enter a new era, as my definition of a serious collector was one who has a collection in four figures.

Most programme collectors can be roughly divided into two camps: obsessive types who keep their collections in chronological order, and obsessive types who keep their collections in alphabetical order. I favoured the former, finding it more efficient. As I counted them, I kept getting distracted, stopping to take a fresh look at a half-forgotten programme, like the Erith and Belvedere against Bromley one that consisted of a single page and failed to carry out the basic function of a programme by leaving both team line-ups blank. Another was Thame United against Ajax (Amsterdam), which was not only the most implausible fixture (it turned out to be the Ajax third team), it also featured the worst cover illustration I had ever seen. It was meant to be a footballer heading a ball, but looked more like the corpse of a murdered Subbuteo player.

After I'd finished counting, I turned my attention to re-reading some of my programme magazines, enjoying hearing from fellow enthusiasts about the themes of their collections. One man collected programmes from matches featuring each league club's record attendance, which meant we had one programme in common, Leeds v. Sunderland in 1967 (attendance 57,892); another collector was coming close to having a pristine programme for every game Derek 'The Doog' Dougan had played in, over five hundred in total from Aston Villa, Everton and Wolves; yet another collector had literally hundreds of local derby programmes from around the world. Mine was nowhere near as coherent: they were mainly either from games I'd been to or had been bought from the Bromley supporters club shop, although I'd also got a few by mail order, and one as a gift.

I can't remember what I dreamt about that night when I finally drifted off to sleep, but I'm pretty sure it had something to do with football programmes.

Work passed slowly the next day, but eventually it was time to go. As I waited for Kevin to come and pick me up for one of the final games in our football marathon, I double-checked my pocket to make sure I had enough change. All the Fourth Division programmes I'd got that season had been 30p. I took three pounds in change, just in case.

The forty-minute drive was one of excited anticipation, although we were both looking forward to different things, and for once we found the ground without getting lost. It wasn't hard to find as it was basically at the end of the M55.

In common with most lower league grounds, the car park was alongside the stadium, which meant only a short walk to the entrance. And, more importantly, the official programme sellers. There were several, but I picked out a young man with ginger hair as it sort of matched his team's shirts.

They say, or at least I imagine they do, that there's nothing like holding your first football programme. Which is almost true. But holding your one thousandth is even more special, as the anticipation is greater. Given the importance of the occasion I'd decided to break with my tradition of buying two, on the grounds that if I had more than one, how would I know which was the thousandth?

My heart was pounding and my stomach churning as I handed him three 10p pieces and, at last, the Blackpool v. Bury programme was mine. The overwhelming sense of achievement I felt was possibly out of proportion to the simple act of buying a programme.

We decided to watch the game from the South Stand, a

rickety old construction, with seats perched on ancient wooden beams. As a tea connoisseur, I was perplexed by the huge advert for ISMAIL & CO., TEA AND COFFEE MERCHANTS BLACKPOOL on the roof of the stand behind the dugouts, as I'd never heard of them. The ground had a slightly decrepit air to it and had clearly seen better days, most of them just after the war, when Matthews and Mortenson used to pack the place out.

The programme wasn't quite as I'd pictured it – an aerial shot of the ground dominated the cover, sandwiched by the fixture's basic information – but my hands were shaking as I opened it. On page three, manager Allan Brown was posing holding a football that had the words MINERVA SUPREME clumsily retouched on to it. I was not surprised to find out on page sixteen that Minerva Supreme supplied the match balls.

Then I saw something that was enough to take my mind off programmes for a few seconds: the sight of Craig Madden, the Great Man who had recently elevated himself to the highest echelon of football gods, running on to the pitch. For someone with more than a passing interest in statistics, his last outing against Northampton had set my pulse racing. His eighteen for the season and eleven in his last seven games put him in the same league as Gerd Müller, the chunky Bayern Munich and West Germany striker who was known as 'Der Bomber', and his famous twenty-three goals in sixteen games.

England had a vital World Cup qualifier coming up against Hungary and I'd managed to convince myself that if Madden continued with his goal spree he'd be an outside chance to make manager Ron Greenwood's squad – assuming he was English, obviously. I envisaged him coming on as a substitute for Kevin Keegan midway through the second half, as they were similar sorts of players. It wasn't that far fetched. Palace's Peter Taylor had played several games for England a few years earlier, when they were in the Third Division.

And what better way to get noticed than by breaking the record for getting to twenty goals in a season faster than anyone else in the division's history?

Madden was in the action straight away, receiving the Minerva Supreme from Steve Johnson and setting up an attack that nearly resulted in the opening goal. With just a minute on the clock came the evening's first hint of drama. Paul Hilton, Bury's huge centre-half, tripped one of the Blackpool strikers as he was closing in on goal. The referee made a fist, held his palm upward and then extended his index finger, bending it several times towards himself, as he summoned Hilton. He lifted the yellow card, put it back in his pocket, then made a fist, put his palm downwards, and rapidly flicked his finger to dismiss the Bury defender from his presence.

I quickly checked the programme, which confirmed what I already knew: Keith Hackett, who I'd seen referee the previous season's Cup Final, was now refereeing a midweek Fourth Division game. His humiliation was completed by the programme editor, who, for the first time in my football watching life, had failed to give the referee's home town. Under 'Officials' it merely said 'Referee K. E. HACKETT'. Thankfully, I already knew that he came from Sheffield.

Then Bury's Pat Howard almost set up the opening goal, with a free kick that Steve Johnson narrowly put wide. Coincidentally, Pat was another one who was celebrating a major milestone that day. This was his 500th league game, which wasn't quite as impressive as my achievement, but was enough to get him presented with a silver salver before the match.

I'd seen Bury so often recently that I no longer needed the programme to help identify Howard or any of the other players. Which was just as well, since I'd been clutching it to my chest for the entire game, as if afraid that someone was going to try and take it away from me. For some reason, even though an important promotion battle was taking place in front of me, and Craig Madden had already come close, I was feeling restless. Initially, I put this down to football fatigue. I'd lost count of the number of games I'd seen in the past three weeks, and all of them were starting to merge into one. Then it dawned on me that I just wanted to go home and luxuriate in the programme, read it from cover to cover before ceremoniously placing it in its shoebox. Shivering away on a cold Wednesday night on the north-west coast watching the league's 70th and 75th best teams cancel each other out seemed a less attractive option.

After a promising start, Craig Madden seemed to be going through a similarly jaded period. He was struggling to put his game in order. The whole crowd seemed subdued. It was a harsh reminder that football doesn't always live up to expectations – a criticism that can rarely be directed at a fixture's programme.

Occasionally, the game flickered into life. Mick Butler put Bury in the lead with a straightforward header from Pat Hilton's cross. The only statistical significance of this goal was that it was the thirteenth time we'd seen Bury score in 197 minutes. I opened my Filofax and used the calculator to work out that this meant a goal every 15.154 minutes, which seemed a very high strike rate. It was something I'd need to research when I got home.

The rest of the half meandered to a halt, and gave Kevin and me a chance to sample Blackpool's tea, presumably supplied by Ismail and Co. It was superb, a credit to the club and the Ismails.

From the way Blackpool's players trotted out for the second half, with their heads bowed, I suspected that the management team (as Allan Brown and Bobby Smith liked to be known) had had stern words. If they had, their midfielder Ronnie Blair had clearly taken note. He took advantage of some terrible Bury defending fifteen minutes before the end to equalize, sending the Minerva Supreme into the net with a lovely left-footer from the edge of the area, but by then I was way beyond caring. I'd got what I came for.

We left before the end, which is something you don't usually do when the scores are level. But we just wanted to get back to a normal life. And, if sitting on your bed reading football programmes until three in the morning is normal, that's exactly what I did. As I'm sure any collector will testify, it's a lot more satisfying going through a thousand programmes than a mere 999.

When Caroline got back the next day, we celebrated with a six-hour *Coronation Street* marathon. I noticed that my concentration was starting to slip by the fifth hour. I apparently hadn't learned my lesson about moderation being the key to enjoyment.

There was no football for me that weekend. Instead, Caroline and I decided to do something different, so we drove to Blackpool, this time courtesy of Ted Rogers. The very same Ted Rogers who hosted the ITV gameshow *3-2-1*, with his sidekick, the hybrid robot/dustbin Dusty Bin. Just before she'd gone away, Caroline and I plus about a dozen diehard *3-2-1* fans from work had gone on an outing to the Palace Theatre to see the Manchester leg of the show's tour. We'd gone because of what was meant to be ironic appreciation of Ted's old-school comedy, but ended up really liking him. Caroline had somehow been convinced to go up on stage, and, thanks to her ability to hold a ping-pong ball between her knees and drop it into a milk bottle, had won a 'Winter Weekend for Two' at the misleadingly named Waldorf Hotel on Blackpool's promenade.

It would be a full two weeks before I went to another football match, England's crucial World Cup qualifier against Hungary. To no one's surprise except mine, Craig Madden didn't make the squad.

FIFA WORLD CUP

QUALIFYING TOURNAMENT GROUP IV

ENGLAND · HUNGARY · NORWAY · RUMANIA · SWITZERLAND

Wednesday 18th November 1981 Kick Off 7.45p.m.

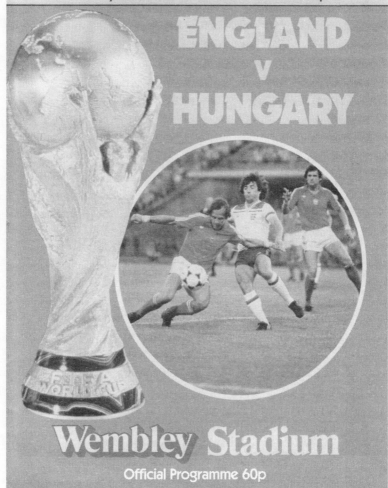

ENGLAND
v
HUNGARY

Wembley Stadium

Official Programme 60p

26

England v. Hungary,
18 November 1981

Kevin Keegan pledges: 'England's players are prepared to spill blood to achieve World Cup qualification tonight.' Ron Greenwood says: 'If we can't go through now, we don't deserve anything.'

From the official programme

1981 was turning out to be a brilliant year to be English. It had started with Bucks Fizz's against-the-odds win in the Eurovision Song Contest, with 'Making Your Mind Up'. It was a victory I felt I'd played a small part in, as I'd been on the jury responsible for selecting the UK entry, thanks to Kevin's contacts in the world of TV. The fact that I voted for another song because the Bucks Fizz one 'wasn't commercial enough' was something I failed to mention when telling people about this.

A few months later was the wedding of Charles and Diana, an event that had captivated my workmates to such an extent that it led to the unusual sight of a group of hardened admen sitting around in an agency with moist eyes as they watched a live broadcast of two strangers getting married. There was even heated discussion about the bride's dress and whether the Emanuels, who had designed it, were right to go with a twenty-five-foot train.

Next it was Ian Botham's turn to contribute to my increasing state of patriotic euphoria, as he beat Australia almost single-handedly to seal the Ashes in the Fifth Test while I watched through binoculars from my office window overlooking the Old Trafford ground.

And now, as I stood alongside Kevin in the South Stand at Wembley on a cold and wet Wednesday night belting out 'Land of Hope and Glory' while the England and Hungary teams walked out of the tunnel, it was destined to get even better. England were just ninety minutes away from qualifying for the 1982 World Cup in Spain.

Most England fans had never heard of any of the Hungarians, but those of us with a keener eye for detail had. I'd taken note (literally) of their goalkeeper, Ferenc Meszaros, when I'd seen him on TV playing for Sporting Lisbon under Big Mal. He'd managed to keep Kevin Keegan's Southampton scoreless in a UEFA Cup tie that night, and my big worry was that he'd continue the tradition of brilliant goalkeeping displays thwarting England's attempts to qualify for World Cups. This was started by Jan Tomaszewski, who was mainly responsible for the traumatic draw with Poland at the same venue eight years earlier, and continued by Italy's Dino Zoff in 1977, also at Wembley, when he stopped the most attacking England side I'd ever seen from getting the goals they needed to get through to Argentina.

Tonight, England were on the verge of earning qualification to a World Cup for the first time in twenty years. And if they succeeded, it would spark a frenzy of activity. A new mascot, to replace World Cup Willie, would be unveiled and would appear on underpants, pyjamas, scarves, vests, rugs ('Step into the

England team') and pillow cases. Someone had leaked a drawing of a heavily jowled cartoon character called Bulldog Bobby to one of the tabloids. I hoped they'd go with something else. I really didn't want a slobbering dog on the front of my underpants. World Cup Willie had been bad enough.

The importance of the occasion was reflected in the size of the crowd. Even though rain was pelting down, Wembley was packed. Every seat was taken and people were still streaming in, desperate to find a vantage point. A row of around thirty middle-aged men, who looked liked anyone's dads, were lined up at the back of the stand. I'd initially thought they were Russian, as most of them were wearing Cossack hats and drinking from flasks, but Kevin pointed out that they were more likely to be Hungarian, given the fixture we were attending. My foreigner stereotyping had let me down. Perhaps if they'd all been playing with Rubik's cubes and eating goulash I might have identified them sooner.

I wasn't the only one to have noticed them. A row of half a dozen England fans in front of us kept looking round and pointing in their direction, muttering among themselves. Given that they had shaven heads and St George flags draped over the backs of their seats, my national stereotyping made me fear the worst.

We all sat back down after 'Land of Hope and Glory', but were soon on our feet again for the national anthem. Normally, this was something I just wanted to get out of the way. But tonight was different. Tonight I was carried away on a wave of patriotic fervour, proud to be an Englishman. I even gave an enthusiastic round of applause to the Duke of Kent as he came out to meet the teams, having discovered a previously unsuspected affection for the Royal Family following Charles and Diana's wedding. I don't think I'd ever loved England as much as I did that year.

With the formalities over, it was down to business. The equation, as England gaffer Ron Greenwood had said before the match, was simple: a win or a draw and England were through; a loss, and they were out. As for Hungary, the result didn't really matter. They were already through.

England's attack had come in for plenty of criticism as they'd managed just five goals in the last seven games. And those had all come from midfield. Despite this, Greenwood had stuck with his 'Dad's Army' line-up, apart from at centre-half, where West Ham youngster Alvin Martin, one of four players in the squad from Greenwood's club side, was preferred to Dave Watson.

The rafters were reverberating with all the cheering and singing, flags were waving, and the English players soon responded. Within a couple of minutes, Kevin Keegan had the game's first real chance when he darted into the area and got on the end of a Coppell cross, but his effort lacked power and Meszaros saved easily.

The next time the Hungarian goalkeeper touched the gleaming white ball, which looked remarkably like a Minerva Supreme, it was to dig it out of his net. A Terry McDermott free kick floated into a packed penalty area. Meszaros went up for it, but Alvin Martin's challenge made him lose control of the ball and it dropped to Trevor Brooking, whose mishit shot looked to be going wide until Paul Mariner, standing by the post, flicked it home. The crowd, including me and Kevin, went berserk, and once again 'Land of Hope and Glory' rang out from all parts of the ground. Mariner's success in front of goal came as no surprise to me. Although he now played for Ipswich, he came from a long line of Plymouth Argyle leading scorers that included Fred Binney and David the Kemp the Kemp the Kemp.

The rest of the first half was almost all England. Peter

Shilton only had one shot to save in the entire forty-five minutes, a weak effort from full-back Balint which he caught easily.

At half time it was a case of so far, so good, and as the Massed Bands of the Royal Marines marched on to the muddy pitch, my thoughts turned to the big dilemma over tonight's programme. As everyone knows, rain is the enemy of the serious collector. When water gets into the pages, they're impossible to separate. Luckily, I'd been aware of the weather forecast and come prepared, bringing a large plastic bag which I sealed my programmes in. Although the temptation to take them out and read them was huge, I knew that in the interests of my collection I had to try and forget all about them until I got home. Even though we were under cover, it could be a disaster if a rogue drop of rain found its way into the bag.

So I did what anyone else would have done. I picked up Kevin's programme when he wandered off for a coffee. Taking a mince pie from my bag (Sainsbury's were doing six for 35p, which confirmed the accuracy of their 'good food costs less at Sainsbury's' slogan), I started reading. When I got to the 'Seen, Heard and Noted' feature, I came across a snippet of information that got my attention.

'It is always an interesting exercise to compare programmes from other countries, particularly when England are the visiting side,' it began. 'The programme for the World Cup match in Oslo was a simple, though extremely neat, black and white production.'

What came next made me sit bolt upright and my heartbeat quicken with desire.

'A weighty 84 pages, with a high ratio of advertising to editorial, it was light on editorial features but packed with lists, charts, results etc. – truly a statistician's delight!'

What I had just read was a description of my dream

programme, more evolved than anything I had seen before. I had to get hold of a copy, but where on earth would I find one? The answer was staring me right in the face. On the opposite page was an advert for David Stacey Publications ('Football Programmes for Programme Collectors'), and almost at the top of their list of programmes for sale was '1981 Norway v. England (WC) £1.50'.

A coincidence? Cynical manipulation of the statistically minded collector? I didn't care. I had to have it, and vowed to get the cheque in the post the minute I got home. I wanted to get in early as I was convinced they wouldn't have enough copies to meet the inevitable demand. This was the game known for Bjørge Lillelien's magnificent commentary ('Lord Nelson! Lord Beaverbrook! Sir Winston Churchill! Sir Anthony Eden! Clement Attlee! Henry Cooper! Lady Diana! Maggie Thatcher! Can you hear me, Maggie Thatcher? Your boys took one hell of a beating! Your boys took one hell of a beating!'), but now it had taken on even greater significance.

As I drifted off into a fantasy about seeing page after page of pie charts in a football programme for the first time, Kevin got back just in time for the start of the second half. His programme, seemingly untouched, lay on his seat where he'd left it.

England were now just forty-five minutes away from Spain, and they started as they'd left off. A thunderous shot from Tony Morley, making his international debut, was tipped over the bar by the busy Meszaros. The Villa man had replaced Coppell, who had looked to have the measure of his marker, Toth, until he was brutally brought down and limped off. A yellow card seemed a small price for the Hungarian full-back to pay. Keegan came close twice; both times he was put through by Brooking, and both times he was thwarted by Meszaros. The visitors had only one further attempt on goal, a rubbish scuffed shot from Laszlo Kiss.

With five minutes left, around ninety-two thousand England fans were whistling, desperately trying to convince the referee that time was up. I tried joining in, and stuck my fingers in my mouth and blew; but however hard I tried, I still couldn't make the whistling sound. It didn't matter as the cacophony was so loud, no one would have noticed the near-silent sound of blowing coming from my lips.

When Monsieur Konrath of France finally signalled full time, no one seemed to want to leave, including the entire England squad who stayed out on the pitch celebrating as much as the crowd. The only movement came from the shaven-headed group in front: they had got out of their seats and were heading towards the Hungarian contingent at the back of the stand. I didn't look round. I didn't want to see what was happening.

After several laps of honour and even more renditions of 'Land of Hope and Glory', the players, who were all now wearing Hungarian shirts (apart from the über-patriotic skipper Keegan), left the field with a final wave. As Kevin and I headed towards the entrance, the announcer gave us the news we'd been hoping for: Northern Ireland and Scotland had also qualified, which made three British teams in next year's World Cup. It was a tournament I couldn't wait to watch on TV.

At the back of the stand, we passed the Hungarian and English fans. They were sharing the flasks and seemed to have temporarily swapped attire, with one of the Hungarians draped in a St George flag and a couple of the shaven-headed Englishmen wisely opting for Cossack hats. It was as good to see as it was unexpected. Outside the stadium, the mood was still one of unconfined joy. No one seemed to be in any rush to get home, and there were large groups standing around singing.

We soaked up the atmosphere. I doubted there would ever be a better time to be English than that night. Qualifying for the

World Cup finals was something a whole generation had never experienced.

Now, England were off to Spain. And while I couldn't wait to watch their progress on TV, I'd also be keeping a close eye on Northern Ireland, and one player in particular.

TESTIMONIAL MATCH
23 NOVEMBER 1981

27

Manchester United v. Manchester United
1977 Cup Winners, 23 November 1981

As friends and admirers of Sammy McIlroy, we, the testimonial committee, take great pleasure in extending a warm and sincere welcome to each and every one of you here this evening.

From the official programme

Taking the lift up to work one July morning earlier that year, half asleep as usual, I'd barely registered who was standing alongside me. When my brain finally woke up and I realized who it was, excitement and panic coursed through me like a caffeine jolt. I tried to talk to him but the words wouldn't come. It's not every day that you find yourself alone in a lift with Sammy McIlroy.

Then things took an even more thrilling turn. When we got to the fourth floor, he followed me into the agency reception area, where he took a seat. Sammy McIlroy, of Manchester United and Northern Ireland, was sitting in the same chair I often sat in while I talked to Connie, the receptionist, instead of working.

I somehow made my way to my desk, which was in a

partitioned-off area I shared with three others, lit up a Sovereign (it was nearly the end of the month and I was broke) and took a sip of the cold black coffee I had left over from the previous afternoon. My colleagues were used to my morning ritual of silently sitting there staring blankly out of the window, so would have been unaware that I was in a state of shock. Eventually, I found my voice.

'You'll never guess who I just came up in the lift with,' I said to Bruce, a lanky Chelsea fan who was unimpressed with anything to do with United.

'Sammy McIlroy?' he said, stifling a yawn.

'How did you know?'

'Just seen him. He'll be here for the meeting.'

'What meeting?'

'The one about his testimonial. We're doing the programme, I think.'

This was my second major bombshell of the morning, and I'd only been awake an hour. Apparently my puzzled expression prompted him to add an explanation of sorts.

'You do know that Win's secretary of the committee, don't you?'

Win, one of our directors, was a United fanatic. She was the one who'd arranged for me to get season tickets. She had become a sort of surrogate mother. I'd spend much of my spare time in her office, talking about football (usually) and advertising (rarely). As I'd only just got back from a fortnight's holiday I'd missed out on the McIlroy news.

I bumped into her just as she was coming out of the meeting, the sort of happy coincidence that happens when you walk past the meeting room about twenty times in the space of half an hour, trying to sneak a peek inside. She filled me in on the testimonial. There was going to be a match at Old Trafford in November between the current United team and the 1977

Cup-winning side, which meant some of the greats from the recent past would be playing. Gordon Hill, my favourite player since George Best, was flying back from Montreal especially for the game. Stuart Pearson, now of West Ham reserves, had also agreed to play, as had Alex Stepney, the best goalkeeper I'd ever seen.

This was something I was desperate to be part of, so I asked if there was anything I could do.

'Well, the agency are taking a full-page ad in the programme – why don't you see what you can come up with? We just want to congratulate Sammy and thank him for ten great years with United.'

Ever since my dad had taken me to my first football match, and I'd seen Johnny Haynes' enthusiastic endorsement of Mettoy Wembley vinyl footballs ('They are reinflatable, repairable, tough and will stand up to any conditions and treatment, and of course are ideal for youngsters'), I'd been fascinated by the advertising in programmes. I loved the way they were often desperate to tie in with football ('We can tackle all your travel arrangements, so kick off your holiday with us'), and they were often the first things I looked for. And now I had the chance to write one, to have it appear in a programme that would be read by tens of thousands of people. To most copy-writers, including all the ones I worked with, this was something to avoid, something at the wrong end of the glamour scale. For them, TV commercials were the ultimate. But not me. Perhaps my love for programmes had distorted my judgement on the importance of the ads they contained, but I couldn't help feeling that my colleagues had their priorities all wrong.

As Caroline was working and wouldn't be home, I decided to work late and try to crack the ad straight away. Alone in the office, I sat down and scribbled a few ideas on an A4 pad, but none was any good. Most followed the well-worn path of abysmal puns. To help me get inspired, I decided to open my bottle of Wilson's Royal Wedding VSP beer, which had been specially brewed to celebrate the marriage of Prince Charles and Lady Diana Spencer. We'd each been given one earlier that day by the brewery, a client of the agency. It seemed a shame to have to tear off the beautiful silver foil covering the cap, but the need for beer overcame any aesthetic concerns. It was delicious. Not only that, it was so strong that I was feeling the effects long before I finished the bottle. This was really good beer. So good that I needed more.

Acting on a hunch, I went into the office of the account director responsible for the Wilson's account, and sure enough, there was a small stash of Royal Wedding VSP bottles concealed under a golf umbrella in the corner. Grabbing a handful, I returned to my desk and got back to work. An hour and several bottles later, the ideas were starting to flow. I was filling page after page with what seemed to be ideas of such brilliance that a string of awards was inevitable. Or they would have been, had there been a category in any of the major award shows for 'Best Programme Advert'.

Headlines were pouring from my pen as the empty bottles piled up, and the more I drank, the easier it became. By one in the morning I reckoned I'd done enough to fill a dozen programmes so I left a pile of paper covered in my scribbles on the desk of Sue, the creative department secretary, with a note asking her to type them out.

I got a taxi home, brimming with pride and excitement, and sleep came easy that night. For once, I wasn't worrying about work. Even though I was acutely aware that Garry Birtles was going through a lean spell, I was utterly confident that I'd now emerged from mine.

Over breakfast the next morning, I discovered that I must

have been a bit more drunk than I thought. Caroline informed me that I'd rung her at work, just before her shift ended at mid-night, sounding flustered and in a panic. She'd thought something was seriously wrong, until I told her why I was call-ing. The conversation had apparently gone a bit like this, before she put the phone down on me:

'Caroline?'

'Yes, what is it? What's the matter?'

'I need a headline for an ad for Sammy McIlroy's testimonial programme – got any ideas?'

'No, I'm a nurse. And I'm working. I'll see you later.'

As Caroline finished telling me about the exchange, some-where, in a far corner of my brain, there was the slightest hint of recognition. And if I'd been so far gone that I'd had a con-versation I barely remembered, wasn't it possible that the lines I'd come up with weren't quite as brilliant as I'd thought at the time?

I had to get to work quickly and find out. As soon as I got there, I saw that Sue had typed my ideas out and left them on my desk, among a mass of screwed-up paper and empty beer bottles. I looked through them. The excitement faded when I realized that what seems a good line after an excess of alcohol can often be meaningless in the cold light of day. Some made no sense at all – what did HOPE YOU MAKE A NET PROFIT TONIGHT SAMMY mean? – while others were plain weak. Our creative director, who had to approve every ad, was prone to dismissing things he didn't like with a 'Desperately poor, David, desperately poor'. I didn't want to give him the opportunity and decided not to bother showing him the vast majority of them.

After throwing away all the ones that were either rubbish or nonsensical, only one survived. I half remembered gazing at an empty bottle of Royal Wedding VSP for inspiration and then scribbling the line PUT A FEW AWAY TONIGHT SAMMY. It wasn't bad. Not as good as I thought it was last night, but not as bad as most of the others.

My anxiety levels were going through the roof as I pushed the headline in front of the creative director, praying that it wasn't going to get the 'desperately poor' treatment. It didn't. He just said, 'This'll do. Don't waste any more time on it,' which was possibly the most positive reaction I'd ever had from him.

I'd done it. My ad was going to be in the programme, taking up a whole page. I rang Caroline with the news and she was happy, knowing how much it meant to me and also because she wouldn't be asked to come up with any further lines.

Watching the programme come together over the following weeks was a fascinating process. I was in Win's office when an envelope arrived from an *Express* journalist who had written about the managers Sammy had worked under. I saw Sue type up Sammy's handwritten message, and stood over one of the artists as he patiently cut out a picture of Sammy with a scalpel and then stuck it to a piece of board with cow gum. Days later, I waited with mounting excitement for the courier to deliver proofs, and sat alongside Jim, the proofreader, as he looked for any mistakes. The revised artwork was then couriered to the printers, who would send the finished programmes direct to Old Trafford.

It was a programme I couldn't wait to hold.

On the morning of the match, I was discussing the prospects with Win and asked her which team would win. To me, the current side looked better on paper, and they were also used to playing together, so I was picking them to edge it 1–0 in a close game. I was shocked when she stated, with a confident smile, that it would be a high-scoring draw, 'something like 4–4 or 5–5, I would think'.

My respect for her football knowledge plummeted. When you've got goalkeepers like Gary Bailey and Alex Stepney, plus defenders of the calibre of Kevin Moran, Martin Buchan, Jimmy Nicholl and John Gidman, there weren't going to be many goals. Especially with the current team topping the First Division table.

She then casually dropped yet another bombshell, revealing that Sammy was going to present her to the teams on the pitch, as he wanted her to be the guest of honour. I asked her to beg Gordon Hill to come back, because he was a genius and I really missed him. I would even leave my wife for him. She just laughed nervously.

Caroline and I had an early dinner at the Azad Manzil, a restaurant we went to so often we no longer had to order; they just brought over her rogan josh, my chicken korma and two glasses of Carlsberg. After we'd eaten, we walked to the ground, arriving just after six. I bought two programmes each (I was half hoping that Caroline might want to start a collection of her own) and we sat down to read them.

We were in the A Stand, which was where the most expensive seats were. We'd turned down the offer of free tickets as this would've defeated the point of a testimonial. Besides, Sammy, who had insisted the prices were kept as low as possible, was Caroline's favourite footballer. Her sole good memory of her visit to Old Trafford had been watching him score a hat-trick, so we both wanted to make a contribution. The crowd wasn't huge, filling only about a third of the stadium. I suspected this was down to a combination of the recession, a freezing cold Monday night and the Altrincham v. Sheffield United Cup replay taking place just down the road.

As I'd already read the programme dozens of times over the previous few weeks, my interest was mainly in page twenty-eight and my ad for the agency. I turned to it straight away, just to make sure there hadn't been any last-minute printing errors. I needn't have worried. I thought it looked fantastic, and Mike, the art director, had done a great job – big black headline over a red background. I was even more thrilled when I imagined Sammy reading it as he sat in the dressing room, waiting to run on to the pitch. I hoped he liked it.

The curtain raiser was Old Trafford's first ever women's match: the Supporters Club Ladies team had a comfortable 3–0 win over a Manchester Division Select XI. This breakthrough in gender equality was slightly dampened when Karen Selby was given the official Man of the Match award.

It was time for the main event. As the teams lined up to be introduced to the guest of honour, it was apparent that the Cup Winners team was on a lower budget, one that didn't stretch to tracksuits. They stood and shivered while the current team stayed warm in their bright red Adidas tops. Then Win, resplendent in fur coat and trademark Su-Pollard-in-*Hi-De-Hi* yellow-framed glasses, tottered on to the pitch in her extravagant heels. Sammy McIlroy introduced her to the players. She looked to be enjoying herself immensely as she moved from legend to legend. I loved it – this was only one step away from being out on the Old Trafford turf myself, shaking hands with my heroes. My pre-match highlight came when Win stopped at Gordon Hill and said something that made him laugh. I allowed myself to think that she was passing on my message.

The Cup Winners took an early two-goal lead, Jimmy Greenhoff getting both from Gordon Hill crosses, before Frank Stapleton pulled one back just before half time. Despite the sparse turnout, there was a festival atmosphere as both teams pushed forward, the crowd cheering for whichever side was attacking. Early in the second half, Bryan Robson equalized, only for Gerry Daly to restore the lead. In the space of a few minutes, the scoreline went from 2–3 to 4–3 when Bryan Robson and then Ray Wilkins gave the current United team the lead. An unexpected substitute, forty-four-year-old Bobby Charlton CBE, came close to making it 5–3, but then Jimmy Greenhoff completed his hat-trick from yet another Gordon Hill pass, and the game ended 4–4. Just as Win had predicted.

It was a brilliant game with an outstanding programme.

At home, it lay casually on the coffee table, open at the PUT A FEW AWAY TONIGHT SAMMY page, for the next few months. Visitors couldn't help but notice it. And if they didn't, I helpfully pointed it out.

That Sammy McIlroy advert proved to be my finest moment at the agency. After over a year there I was getting restless and started to look around, but other Manchester agencies failed to show any interest. When Caroline first mentioned the idea of moving, I think she probably meant 'let's move back to Leeds or maybe to London', not 'let's move halfway around the world to a country where we don't know anyone'. But after trying half a dozen headhunters (or 'executive search consultants' as they had taken to calling themselves), I managed to land the grand total of one interview.

And that was for a job in New Zealand.

LEE**DS**

LEEDS UNITED AFC

OFFICIAL MATCHDAY
PROGRAMME No. 19
PRICE 30p

LEAGUE DIVISION ONE
Saturday 3rd April 1982
MANCHESTER
UNITED

MATCH SPONSORS
Radio Aire
362

28

Leeds United v. Manchester United, 3 April 1982

All the supporters should remember that they represent Leeds United and any misbehaviour might result in very serious consequences for the club that could, in the end, affect all supporters.

From the official programme

We had forty-eight hours to decide our entire future.

I was offered the job in New Zealand on a Friday afternoon and they wanted an answer by first thing Monday morning. This sent my anxiety levels rocketing, and I reverted to my default behaviour in times of extreme stress. There was a time when this would have meant rolling a dice and slavishly following the outcome, but now I relied on list-making. The idea was that Caroline and I would instantly see whether the benefits of moving outweighed the benefits of staying. Frustratingly, like Sammy McIlroy's testimonial the previous year, it ended as a high-scoring draw.

There was only one thing for it. To run away. So I suggested we go and spend the weekend in Leeds with Caroline's sister, who lived near Elland Road. That way we could talk things through without any distractions.

The main problem seemed to be our limited knowledge of New Zealand. From my time as a statistician, I knew its chief exports were milk, butter and cheese. I knew the first man to climb Everest came from there. And I knew they were quite good at rugby. Possibly not enough information on which to base a life-changing decision, but a lot more than I knew about, say, Andorra.

By Saturday morning the scales were tilting slightly in favour of staying. This was influenced, in part, by reading the *Yorkshire Post*'s preview of the game that afternoon between Leeds United and Manchester United, the two big teams I'd supported since moving up north – although Bromley's (usually disapointing) result was still the first one I looked for in the paper. As Caroline and I were both exhausted from all the to-ing and fro-ing, we decided to take advantage of the astonishing coincidence of this game taking place just 2.2 miles away from where we were staying.

I'd seen both reserve teams in action at Old Trafford a fortnight earlier and it was one of the best games of the season. I'd gone because it was Gordon McQueen's comeback after two months out through injury and I wanted to monitor his progress, but it was the young Leeds reserves goalie, David Seaman, whose deeds took up more space in the notebook section of my Filofax, as he made stunning saves from Alan Davies and sixteen-year-old Norman Whiteside.

As Caroline and I walked down Elland Road and I caught sight of the programme seller, I wondered how I could ever even think about leaving England behind. A feeling that was magnified as I perused the Leeds United Official Matchday Programme No. 19 while standing in the queue at the ticket office. The first thing I noticed was that John Lukic, whom young Seaman would have to dislodge if he ever wanted to play first-team football, had been presented with a Philips hostess trolley for his recent Man of the Match performance against Forest. I loved his slightly embarrassed fixed grin as he awkwardly posed with possibly the least manly Man of the Match prize in football history. No wonder programmes were my passion. They probably didn't even have them in New Zealand, except for games of rugby.

We'd arrived at the ground about an hour before kick-off, and managed to get tickets in the South Stand. It was Caroline's first visit to Elland Road and my ninth. What I hadn't told my Leeds supporting friends was that I'd never seen Leeds win at home – a statistical improbability so great that the odds on it happening were astronomical. I knew this because I'd actually worked them out during an unproductive morning at work.

Although I was clearly a jinx on them – since I'd been watching them they'd gone from being a top-of-the-table side to relegation favourites – I really enjoyed the Leeds brand of football. In Frank Worthington they had one of the game's real characters, one of the last of the old-fashioned mavericks. When I'd shaved off my Garry Birtles beard I'd left the moustache as a tribute to Worthington. In a few days' time, according to the programme, he would be opening a new branch of his sports and leisurewear chain in Bradford and if you went along to the grand opening at four p.m. you could meet him, as well as Peter Barnes, Trevor Cherry and Paul Hart. I took out my Filofax and noted that down, just in case I happened to find myself in Bradford late on Thursday afternoon.

The South Stand was packed to the point that we were unable to move, and United had brought a huge amount of support. Some of the home fans had infiltrated the area where we were standing, which meant that the atmosphere was incredibly hostile, with small groups of rival supporters who notoriously hated each other only yards apart in places. The two sets of fans clearly weren't interested in watching the game as they were facing each other, screaming threats, and separated only by thin lines of police.

It was a particularly bad year for hooliganism, which frequently made the front pages of the tabloids, and it wasn't long before fights were breaking out all around us. The police seemed hopelessly outnumbered. There were children clutching on to their dads' sleeves, terrified by what was going on around them. I'd been to plenty of matches where there was crowd trouble, but this was the first time I'd felt in danger. I was even more worried about Caroline and asked if she wanted to go home, half hoping she'd say yes, but she said she was fine. She'd always been braver than me. You have to be when you work in the casualty ward. She saw this kind of thing most nights and every Saturday afternoon.

When the action finally switched to the pitch, what we saw was an extremely entertaining match-up between two sides determined to put on a show, with plenty of goals and great saves. Unfortunately, that was the curtain-raiser penalty shoot-out between Radio Aire from Leeds and Manchester's Piccadilly Radio. The main event was a different story.

It started badly with the news that Birtles wouldn't be playing and that Scott McGarvey would replace him, forming a bubble-permed duo with Bryan Robson. Both sides needed three points to lift them beyond the fringe – of the relegation zone in Leeds' case and of the title hunt in United's. The game started slowly and cautiously, with Leeds' young midfield pairing of Gwyn Thomas and Terry Connor blunting the effect of United's £3 million pair Ray Wilkins and Bryan Robson. It would have been a hard match to enjoy even if the football had been flowing, but combined with the atmosphere in the ground I was tense and had that butterflies-in-the-stomach feeling.

The realization was starting to dawn that I'd been looking for reasons to stay in England and I'd been convincing myself that football was the key, impossible to leave behind because it was always brilliant. The reality was different. I'd seen plenty of rubbish games, and this was another of them.

One of the main things we'd discussed when trying to decide whether or not to move was starting a family. We both wanted kids, and as I looked around I saw everything that made bringing them up in England, however much we loved the place, seem like a bad idea – the violence, the overcrowding, the boredom, the lousy weather. I glanced over at Caroline and I could see she was feeling what I was thinking. For the first time, New Zealand became not just something to fantasize about over a bottle of wine and several lists, but a really appealing option.

This feeling was heightened by what continued to happen on the pitch, which was next to nothing. The game just never got going. It was scrappy and uninspiring, with no shape – and these were two of the biggest clubs in the country. The highlights were few and far between. United's Steve Coppell was responsible for most of them, as he twice hit the bar and then forced Lukic into a spectacular one-handed save.

The start of the second half showed brief promise, when Connor made a great tackle to deny Remi Moses, and a few minutes later Frank Stapleton burst through, but his shot went just past the post. The closest Leeds came to scoring was when a Hird cross was fumbled by Gary Bailey, but Buchan headed off the line.

Neither side deserved to win, and when Mr J. Hunting (Leicester) mercifully blew his whistle for full time, the players were booed off the field.

Outside the ground the fighting continued, and cars were

being overturned. The police, once again, were nowhere to be seen. To make sure people knew I was a committed part of the punk movement I was wearing a black T-shirt with ANARCHY IN THE UK spray-painted across the front. Now that I was witnessing it first hand, I was less keen on the idea.

It was a massive relief to find our car in one piece and to get on the M62 back to Manchester. By the time we got home we had made a firm decision: I'd be taking the job and we would be moving to Wellington in around eight weeks' time. We were going to give it a go for two years and then come back if it wasn't working out.

My bedtime reading that night was meant to be the *Lonely Planet Guide to New Zealand*, followed by that day's Leeds v. Manchester United programme. But as it represented such a huge moment in our lives, I decided to start with the programme. Although Caroline tended to be less sentimental about them than I was, I felt sure that this one would eventually mean as much to her as it did to me. It looked as though it could be the last one I ever bought, the end of an era.

Thankfully, it was a stunning example of the art form and the best that Bob Baldwin, the Leeds programme editor, had produced while I'd been going to Elland Road. The things that make a great programme, to me, are massive doses of statistical information, good action and off-field photography, eye-catching design and outstanding adverts. As I studied the programme in detail, it became increasingly apparent that Baldwin had pulled out all the stops to put together his best of the season. This was an editor at the top of his game. The opposition information was thrillingly detailed (I hadn't known that more of United's current squad were born in Edinburgh than any other city), the cover shot of Arthur Graham scoring against Forest was a gem, the articles were beautifully written and varied, and the adverts, which included a brilliant one for

Distinct Upholstery (starring Eddie Gray and his wife Linda), were outstanding.

If this was going to be my last ever programme, I couldn't have asked for more.

I gave in my notice on the Monday morning, and after work we celebrated our upcoming move with dinner at our favourite restaurant, the Azad Manzil in Chorlton. Due to a slight breakdown in communication (they got the impression we were leaving that night), we received a tearful farewell from the manager and waiters who wished us luck in our new life overseas and insisted that we didn't pay for our meals. This was especially embarrassing as we went back a couple of nights later and they clearly believed we'd carried out an elaborate scam.

One of the toughest things about going was having to leave Sid, our cat, behind. We'd originally decided to take him with us and had even started filling all the forms in when we realized that it wouldn't be right to put him through a long, loud and scary flight, several injections, quarantine for a month, and unfamiliar surroundings just to make us feel better. So when we rented our house out to a bunch of students, we were delighted when they offered to adopt Sid and promised to keep us updated with his progress.

The goodbyes were every bit as hard as I'd imagined. I was really going to miss my mum and dad. I'd got into the habit of driving down to Bromley every couple of months to see them and, despite having moved away and got married, it always felt like going home. My dad, especially, seemed to be proud that I was managing to carve out a career, and I always brought my latest ads with me, hoping he'd like them.

Leaving my parents, as well as our friends and Sid, was made slightly easier by the knowledge that it wouldn't be long before I saw them all again. We'd been promised flights home every couple of years.

On the way to the airport there was still one nagging doubt I hadn't been able to shake off. Rugby was huge in New Zealand, everyone knew that, but what was their domestic football like? Their national team had made it to the World Cup, but there had been a distinct lack of big-name opponents along the way. I'd never heard a thing about club football in the country, or about any supporters of it. Would they even have a Football League equivalent over there?

ROTHMANS

WORLD CUP
BUILD-UP SERIES

NEW ZEALAND v WATFORD

QEII Park, Christchurch
Sunday 23rd May 1982

Athletic Park, Wellington
Wednesday 26th May 1982

Mt Smart Stadium, Auckland
Saturday 29th May 1982

NEW ZEALAND FOOTBALL ASSOCIATION INC.

OFFICIAL SOUVENIR PROGRAMME $1

29

New Zealand v. Watford,
26 May 1982

It is with much pleasure that we welcome the famous Watford
Football Club to New Zealand. Not only does it derive its fame
from Elton John but also on the playing field.

From the official programme

Caroline and I flew out of Heathrow in the late spring of 1982
and arrived in New Zealand about twenty years earlier. At least
that was how it seemed. Everything – the fashion, the haircuts,
the cars – was from the distant past.

After sleepwalking through customs, where they seemed
more concerned about finding fruit or cakes than drugs or
weapons (perhaps their social problems were different from
ours), we got our first major shock. Before we could get on the
connecting plane from Auckland to Wellington we had to walk
– yes, *walk* – to another airport. This was my first inkling that
New Zealanders like to do things a little differently.

After lugging most of our worldly possessions for a mile or
two on the coldest morning I could remember since my days
of doing a paper round, we finally got there. Confused and

disorientated, I asked a smiling woman in an Air New Zealand uniform where we had to go to get the Wellington flight.

'Over there at the chicken,' she said, pointing to a counter where no chicken was visible.

'The chicken?' I asked.

'Yis, the chicken,' she confirmed.

Caroline tapped me on the arm and pointed to the sign saying CHECK IN, and the penny dropped. The accent was going to take a bit of getting used to.

After we'd chicked in, we had a couple of hours to spare before boarding so we decided to sample some New Zealand airport food and read some of the local papers. The choice of where to start was made easier when I discovered there was only one local paper on sale, the *New Zealand Herald*.

Having stayed awake for the entire flight, I was fighting exhaustion and struggling to avoid dropping off to sleep. The last time I'd stayed awake for more than twenty-four hours was the time I hitched to Southampton to watch George Best. Thankfully, those days of going to ridiculous lengths just to watch a football match were long gone.

Or so I thought.

Turning straight to the back page of the *Herald*, I skipped over the rugby news to where a small paragraph had caught my eye. First Division Watford were playing New Zealand in Wellington that very afternoon. This was barely believable. We were about to fly into a city where John Barnes, Luther Blissett and Nigel Callaghan would be playing. Perhaps my big fear about rugby being the only sport anyone ever watched was unfounded. This was such a thrilling breakthrough that I was puzzled when Caroline showed no interest in going to the game, preferring the option of sleeping. But I suddenly felt re-energized. It was as though the football gods had put on a special welcome for me in my new country. Sleep would have to wait. I'd never travelled twelve thousand miles to watch a game before.

'Are you sure you don't want me to stay with you?' I asked Caroline.

'Absolutely.'

'Are you *sure*?'

'Yes, really. Just go. Please. I want you to go.'

For a fleeting moment I wondered if having had me witter away at her and nervously cling on to her arm for the past day and a bit had left her wanting a bit of time on her own.

We touched down in Wellington forty-five minutes before kick-off, and soon found a taxi. I was confident about getting to the ground in time, but that soon changed when it became apparent that the ride was going to be a horrendously slow one, especially on even the slightest of uphill gradients, where 'slow' became 'barely moving at all'. The thought of another twenty-six hours trapped inside a metal box while an important game of football took place without me prompted me to ask the driver if there was anything wrong with the engine. 'It's running on LPG, mate,' he said, by way of explanation. When pushed, he told me that LPG was an alternative fuel that saved him thousands of dollars a year and the planet from a premature demise. I was all for saving the environment, as long as it didn't get in the way of me watching football.

As if to signal that the conversation was over, he switched on a little transistor radio that was dangling from the sun visor. I was delighted to hear the familiar sounds of the Human League's current single 'Don't You Want Me?' coming out of it. I'd been a bit worried about what kind of music the locals listened to, so this was reassuring.

After we dropped Caroline off at the motel and I'd carried our bags inside, I got to Athletic Park, which was better known for rugby, with seconds to spare. It was a smallish stadium at the top of a steep hill (which took about five minutes for the taxi to crawl up), exposed on all sides, and it looked absolutely packed, despite it being a Wednesday afternoon. But then New Zealand's first ever appearance in the World Cup was just over a fortnight away – they would be facing Scotland in Malaga – and the locals had turned out in force to see them off. It warmed my heart to see youngsters excitedly scurrying past, clutching their programmes. I was starting to feel at home already.

You never expect the best seat when you turn up moments before kick-off as most people have either got there early or booked in advance, but the one I'd landed myself with was nothing short of terrifying. After entering the ground and buying myself two cups of black coffee, I was pointed in the direction of the Millard Stand, the only place where there was spare seating. It soon became clear why Wellingtonians considered it a last resort. I had to climb a sheer face to reach the first available seat, which was near the top of the uncovered stand, which seemed to be built on thin and visibly rusty steel girders. Not only was it incredibly steep, I also had to struggle into the face of a gale-force wind. No wonder New Zealanders were known for their climbing. When I finally got to my seat I flopped down, exhausted.

Any thoughts of relaxation were soon replaced by sheer terror. It was an unusual experience clinging desperately to a seat that was swaying violently, feeling sure that if I lost my grip I would fall hundreds of feet. I was far too petrified to concentrate on the players as they trotted on to the pitch, although I couldn't help but notice that luxuriant facial hair, which had more or less disappeared from the English game, was sprouting freely here. Slug-like moustaches adorned all but a few of the home team, and the full beard was also very much in evidence.

Fortunately, the programme helped me take my mind off the

precarious position I had found myself in. This particular publication was something I had mixed feelings about. On one hand, I hadn't been expecting a programme at all, so it felt good to have one I'd bought in another country in my collection at last. On the other hand, it was giving me an early confirmation of the relaxed and loose Kiwi attitude I'd heard so much about. They'd produced one programme to cover the three games with Watford in the grandly named 'Rothmans World Cup Build-Up Series', even though they were all in different cities. The team page was fairly pointless, as it listed eighteen Watford players and twenty-one from New Zealand.

There was some good stuff, though. I discovered that eleven of the New Zealand squad had been born in Britain and that Watford's assistant manager was former Arsenal gaffer Bertie Mee, who once got me to sing at Highbury. Of even more interest, however, was the advertising. I was keen to get an idea of the standard in New Zealand and was secretly delighted to see a full-page advert for Rank Xerox with a slightly puzzling headline claiming that THE ONLY COPIER THAT IS JUST AS GOOD AS A XEROX IS ANOTHER XEROX COPIER. The prospect of starting a new job as an advertising copywriter in a new country in less than five days' time suddenly felt a lot less intimidating.

The advice generally given to those of us with a fear of heights is not to look down, but as that would have defeated the point of being there I forced myself to focus on what was taking place on the distant patch of green below. I was soon so wrapped up in the game that my discomfort and near total exhaustion were quickly forgotten.

It didn't take me long to become a passionate All Whites (as the New Zealand football side was known) fan. I've always gone for the underdog, and I loved reading about how my new team had come through a record fifteen qualifying games to get to Spain. Their journey had taken them to Kuwait and Saudi

Arabia, Indonesia and Taiwan, China and Australia, Fiji and Singapore. The team's spirit was evident as they took the game to Watford. Grant Turner, the tattooed Kiwi midfielder, made a ferocious tackle on Nigel Callaghan ('a fast ball-playing forward') which probably would have merited a red card in England, but this was New Zealand, where men were men, so the referee ignored it completely. Wynton Rufer, the home team's '19-year-old exciting prospect' then put a lovely cross in from the right, which Steve Wooddin poked home with what the ground announcer called his 'lethal left foot'. All around me people were jumping up and down and punching the air with excitement. The stand was shaking so much that it felt as though it would topple over at any moment.

Watford came back and their forward line looked especially threatening, Barnes, Blissett and Callaghan giving the All Whites' defence a torrid time. At just after 2.25 in the morning according to my watch (I'd forgotten to change it to New Zealand time), Callaghan's cross hit Kenny Cresswell on the arm and Mr G. Fleet (Auckland) pointed to the spot. Blissett, the first black player to score for England, sent keeper Richard Wilson the wrong way and it was 1–1.

By now the action was swinging from end to end, and I was lost in the excitement. There was more to come, including a stunning drive from thirty yards out by one of the Kiwis, which produced a great save from Eric Steele, and Grant Turner heading against the Watford bar towards the end. Then the whistle went for full time, and having seen my adopted country hold First Division Watford to a creditable draw, I made the long climb back to earth, happy that football was alive and well in New Zealand.

Around this time my brain suddenly seemed to shut down and I began to feel delirious. A combination of nearly thirty hours travelling without sleep, a short mountain climb, sitting so high that oxygen deprivation was a real possibility, and an emotionally draining football match can do that. I had a slight panic when I forgot the name of the motel, but luckily it was printed on the key-ring. On the way there I saw a ginger cat and my heart almost burst with happiness: Sid had somehow followed us to New Zealand! As I ran over to him, it dawned on me that it was an older and fatter cat that bore only the slightest resemblance to Sid. I felt crushed.

When I got back to the motel, sleep came easily.

My first day at work provided more reassurance that rugby wasn't the only game in town, when I rounded a corner and suddenly found myself face to face with Tommy Hutchison of Manchester City. Or at least a shorter, rounder version. I hoped this wasn't going to be another case of mistaken identity, but suspected it was.

'You look just like—' I started.

'Tommy Hutchison?' he finished. 'I get that a lot. He's my cousin.'

It didn't take long for us to become friends, and we spent the next hour talking football, particularly his famous relative's part in that Spurs v. Manchester City Cup Final, and New Zealand's chances in the upcoming World Cup. His name, inevitably, was Dave, so in the interests of avoiding confusion we agreed that I'd refer to him as Birrell and he'd call me Roberts. Less inevitably, he was a Raith Rovers fan.

Getting on so well with him made it easier to settle in at the agency. It wasn't that much different from my last job, apart from the standard of work being terrible. This meant that any time I wrote a semi-coherent ad, one that would have merited a 'desperately poor' in Manchester, it was greeted with awe in Wellington, where words like 'genius' were tossed around. I loved working there.

I was also loving New Zealand, especially when the World

Cup kicked off and rugby was all but forgotten. For the All Whites' first game a large proportion of the population tuned into their TVs at eight in the morning. Birrell and I watched the match at work with around thirty colleagues, and the roar that greeted Steve Sumner's scrambled goal ten minutes into the second half made the hairs on my neck stand on end. It was even louder when Steve Wooddin added a barely believable second with what the whole country now seemed to refer to as his 'lethal left foot', just nine minutes later. The fact that Scotland got five really didn't matter.

A week later I was lying on the couch at home, getting myself ready for the *really* big one, New Zealand against Brazil in the final pool game. I'd been having quite a few severe headaches recently which the doctor assured me were nothing to worry about, but they were bad enough for me to prefer to stay at home and watch the game rather than see it at work with a bunch of noisily enthusiastic colleagues.

Despite having lost to the Scots and then going down 3–0 to the USSR, this was a chance for the All Whites to take on what the papers misguidedly called 'the soccer equivalent of the All Blacks'. My preparation consisted of re-reading the Watford programme and using the profile pages to pick my starting eleven. I was just studying the write-up on Steve Wooddin, where his left foot was wrongly described as 'deadly' instead of 'lethal', when Caroline strolled through the door, a mysterious smile on her face.

'Congratulations,' she said, before adding six words that instantly made me forget about the programme in my hand, as well as the World Cup: 'You're going to be a dad.'

THE T⚽DAY LEAGUE
DIVISION ONE

Saturday, January 24th 1987
Kick-off 3.00 p.m.

Tottenham Hotspur

Sponsored by **HOLSTEN**

80p

ASTON VILLA

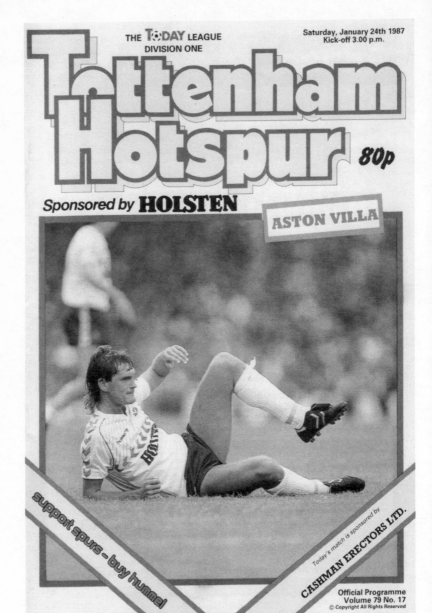

support spurs - buy hummel

Today's match is sponsored by
CASHMAN ERECTORS LTD.

30

Tottenham Hotspur v. Aston Villa,
24 January 1987

Have you joined the Spurs members club yet? It is your chance
to get close to the club for an annual subscription of just £5.

From the official programme

While New Zealand was a great place to live, it had its draw-
backs, the main one being the calibre of football programmes.
When you've got used to collecting ones from FA Cup Finals
and England World Cup qualifiers, it's a real culture shock
being forced to accumulate four- and eight-page publications
from games like Wellington Diamond United v. Raumati
Hearts in the Chatham Cup and Miramar Rangers v. Napier
City Rovers in the Air New Zealand League.

But now I was about to get my hands on a proper First
Division programme again. We were back in England on a brief
visit, which was mainly designed to show off our three-year-old
daughter, a beautiful and good-natured girl who had been
named after a TV programme. More specifically, the TV programme about a private detective called Hazell, which had been
created by Terry Venables, the QPR manager. Caroline and I

had been watching it together when her waters broke and we rushed to hospital. Fifteen hours later, our very own Hazel was born.

After experiencing the unexpectedly moving sight of my mum and dad embracing Hazel for the first time, I managed to make a deal with Caroline. I could watch one football match while we were in the country, as long as I promised to stop going on about all the football I was missing. My first thought was to make a triumphant return to Hayes Lane and watch the 1987 version of Bromley, but with typically poor planning, we'd managed to arrive at the start of a four-week period when they didn't have a home game, and would be leaving the day before Dulwich Hamlet's visit.

Looking through the fixture list for the only Saturday when nothing had been planned, I decided that Spurs against Aston Villa seemed the most promising game – an exciting, attacking team at home to one with easily the worst defence in the division. Villa had conceded an average of over two goals a game and had won only one of their last fourteen. Spurs, meanwhile, were only a point outside the top four and had Clive Allen, top scorer in the entire league with twenty-three.

One of the game's added attractions was Steve Hodge. He'd left Villa for Spurs a month before, claiming that playing for a relegation-threatened team was harming his England chances. In the paper that morning, Spurs manager David Pleat was worried that the emotion of the occasion could get to Hodge and that his all-action style could get him into trouble against his former club. To make the point even clearer, Pleat added his opinion that 'Steve is certainly no fairy'.

As I walked along White Hart Lane, there was one thing I wanted to see more than anything else. The official programme seller. And I could barely believe the sight that greeted me outside the ground. There were swarms of them. Programmes had obviously become more popular since I'd been away. I picked one out and felt a huge surge of excitement as I handed over £1.60 for two programmes. It had been too long since I'd experienced this thrill and I'd forgotten how powerful it was.

Then I looked at the cover and my heart sank. Something had changed in the time I'd been away. As I flicked through it, the Spurs programme felt more like a sales booklet, almost every page trying to sell something. The cover somehow managed to cram four companies on to it in different places: Today (league sponsors), Holsten, Hummel and Cashman Erectors Ltd. In case you missed the point, there was a picture of Glenn Hoddle, whose shirt featured the Holsten and Hummel logos prominently. It seemed that football had fully embraced the spirit of Thatcherism.

Inside the programme, various players had been co-opted to help boost sales for various sponsors. Poor Ossie Ardiles, who seemed to be a man of quiet dignity, had been forced to don a hideous pink sweatshirt ('Are you a loyal Spurs supporter? Well, tell the world!'), which could be yours for £14.95 + p&p. And for those with bigger budgets, the centre pages offered a trio of younger and less recognizable players modelling a range of spectacularly ugly New Direction Leisuresuits. The ones wearing the yellow and blue versions looked a lot happier than the glum young man who had drawn the short straw and been given the pink one. These would cost you £47.90 apiece.

For the loyal fan, it would be hard to know what to buy first.

Then there was the Spurs club ('the club for REAL supporters'), which offered membership for just £5. And if you were too young for that, you could join Junior Spurs (membership also £5). Buying tickets for the next game at White Hart Lane, a cup tie against Crystal Palace, now meant paying a 'booking fee' to an agency.

The game had changed. I knew that every time I picked up

the programme to re-read it, which would be often, it would remind me of the exact time I realized that football was no longer a game, it was a business.

If more confirmation of this were needed, it was provided by page eighteen, which had nothing but eighty-one company logos on it, and no further explanation. These ranged from huge multinationals like ICI and Tesco to smaller local outfits like J. Barr (Finchley). Given the new direction football seemed to be going in, I wasn't surprised that the price of a seat, as well as a programme, had just about trebled since I'd last been to a match in England.

But at least the seat (£9) was a good one, near the halfway line, facing the dugouts. I felt a real thrill seeing the players run out, some I'd seen before, like Glenn Hoddle, and others I'd only seen on TV, like Tony Daley and Chris Waddle. As they warmed up, I noticed something odd. The hoardings around the ground seemed to be aimed at Tottenham's little-known Scandinavian (or possibly German) fan-base. Behind Clemence's goal was an advert for PKVINNARKONO. Opposite me was one for HASSE! mineral water. Looking around, I saw a host of unfamiliar names like MELKA, KOMEILOTT and RAMLOSA.

Obviously not everyone in London had been as desperate to watch a football match as me – the ground couldn't have been more than half full. Even so, I was feeling a little uneasy – something I'd noticed when I was in biggish crowds. When I'd mentioned this to Caroline she hadn't thought it unusual, adding, somewhat unnecessarily, that it was just as well I was a Bromley fan, as big crowds weren't something I'd ever have to worry about.

At least I wasn't in the Villa end, which looked packed. They were singing a song that indicated disagreement with David Pleat's assertion that Hodge was no fairy. From the home fans' end came a constant chant of 'Come on you Spurs!'

As a keen observer of football fashion, I took note of several things: the claret and blue wristbands sported by a couple of the Villa players; Spurs' shorts, which were the tightest I'd seen since Wham's 'Wake Me Up Before You Go-Go' video; and the all-white Hummel tracksuit ensemble worn by the ballboys. I felt confident that all of these items would be available to buy somewhere. This was also true of the music coming over the speakers. As The Housemartins' single 'Caravan of Love' faded, DJ Willie Morgan helpfully pointed out that it was available at 'Our Price Records all over London and the rest of England'.

With the commercials out of the way, it was time for some football. And it didn't take long for one player to stand out. I knew Glenn Hoddle was meant to be good, but what you saw on TV couldn't prepare you for just how influential he was. Despite a knee injury, he seemed to be everywhere, doing plenty of running off the ball. One nonchalant thirty-yard pass to Nico Claesen was so inch-perfect and unexpected that I immediately forgot my disappointment with all the commercialization and remembered why I loved football in the first place.

Steve Hodge, whose popularity among the Villa fans was on the low side after criticizing the team's lack of ambition and adventure, provoked a further breakdown in relations in the thirteenth minute when he got the ball by the MOBIRA sign on the left, cut inside and beat Nigel Spink at the near post to give Spurs the lead. As was my habit, I looked for my Golden Goal number in the programme. There wasn't one. Why would there be? There was no money in it for the club.

And that was the highlight of the opening forty-five minutes. After a satisfactory half-time pie (60p), cup of tea (30p) and leisurely read of the programme (80p), it was time for the second half.

Spurs always looked more likely to score, but it took them a surprisingly long time to increase their lead. But when they did, it was a goal to remember.

Headed goals from corners rarely stick in the mind, but the one Hodge got not long after the restart was so perfect I would later buy a video of the Spurs season (£9.99 + p&p) just so I could see it again. And again and again. Hoddle took the corner, and Hodge timed his run beautifully to the edge of the six-yard box, where he outjumped the much taller Martin Keown. His powerful header found the top left-hand corner before Steve Hunt on the line had even had a chance to move. For reasons I didn't fully grasp, this inspired the Spurs fans to start singing 'Tottenham one, Arsenal nil, Hallelujah'.

The home side sealed the victory ten minutes from the end. Hoddle played a perfect ball to Claesen, who looked several yards offside when he slotted the ball home, but the young linesman, Mr Graham Poll (Herts), had kept his yellow flag down and the goal was allowed. A chant of 'Ni-co, Ni-co, Ni-co, Ni-co' went up, which made more sense than the reaction to the previous goal, and Spurs had the game sewn up. Hoddle almost added a fourth a few minutes later, with an audacious chip that Spink just managed to get a hand to.

By the time the final whistle went, the crowd had shrunk to next to nothing, which surprised me. Perhaps the Spurs supporters had flights to Helsinki or Stockholm to catch. I'd stayed until the end because anyone who had studied the programme closely would have learned that Villa conceded most goals between the seventy-sixth and ninetieth minutes. I felt that witnessing Claesen's goal, which fell within that time-frame, was a suitable reward for my attention to statistical detail.

As I walked away from the ground, I came across the official club shop in Park Lane. I couldn't resist popping inside. Five minutes later I came out with an official authorized Spurs calendar which had cost me £2. I managed to resist the lure of the pink Hummel sweatshirt as worn by Ossie Ardiles, which had managed the distinction of looking even more hideous in real life than it did in the programme.

The next day we went up to Manchester, the highlight being an emotional reunion with Sid the Cat. Emotional for me and Caroline, that is. He didn't recognize either of us.

After that it was time for the long journey back to New Zealand.

On the plane, I managed to read every single one of the Sunday papers. In one of them there was an article which said that some of the bigger clubs, including Spurs, were threatening to form a breakaway league unless they were given a bigger slice of the TV revenue. Although I couldn't see this happening, it was yet another sign that things were changing in football.

When we got home, I added the programme to my collection and wondered how long it would be before we went back for another one. Before the trip, I hadn't seen my mum and dad in four and a half years, and I definitely didn't want to leave it that long before I saw them again.

Later that year, our family grew with the birth of a son, Billy, who came along on a Christian Feast Day (according to my Spurs calendar). As we entered the new decade, Frank completed the hat-trick (bizarrely, also born on a Christian Feast Day according to the calendar). Contrary to popular belief, they weren't named after West Ham players from the seventies, even if Billy Bonds and Frank Lampard both appeared in the West Ham v. Hereford programme, which I often re-read.

I loved being a family man. I'd always felt a strong sense of envy when looking at the players' 'off duty moments' in programmes, where they posed with their wife and kids, accompanied by blurb like 'How time flies! Asa Hartford must have many reasons for thinking along those lines, not least of all as his happy young family keep growing.' And now it was happening to me.

Life was the best it had ever been. A wife I adored, three children I loved so much that I couldn't wait to rush home to them every night, and a recent promotion at work, where I was now the youngest director in the company's history.

I was in my mid thirties and I had everything to look forward to.

Winfield SOCCER

NEW ZEALAND
V
ENGLAND

MT SMART STADIUM 3 JUNE 1991
ATHLETIC PARK WELLINGTON 8 JUNE 1991

NZFA
CENTENARY
1891 ▶ 1991

Winfield
94's THE AIM

31

New Zealand v. England,
8 June 1991

The England squad for the two match series with the All
Whites is probably the most formidable collection of football
talent to ever play in this country.

From the official programme

Twenty-one years after that visit to White Hart Lane, it seemed
as though my entire house was covered in programmes. I had
over a thousand of them spread out over every square inch of
floorspace in the living room, corridor and spare bedroom.
They were on tables, chairs, even on top of the TV. Somehow
I had to pick out the thirty or so that were the most important
to me, as Liz, my second wife, and I were flying out to a new
life in the US and there was limited room in the luggage.

I'd always had a habit of saving the best until last, such as
eating everything on my plate before demolishing the chips,
and now I was applying the same principle to packing.
Everything was now done except the most important thing. We
were leaving in ninety-six hours and it was time to make the
final programme selection.

My strategy was to make an informed decision by reviewing the entire collection before making the final choice. This was going well until Liz came into the living room and found me lying on the floor engrossed in a Manchester City v. Northampton programme from 1981. She rather unfairly accused me of reading them instead of doing the job I was supposed to be doing.

As time ticked by, a few easy choices helped lower my anxiety levels. And from the moment I made my very first tentative shortlist, New Zealand v. England from 1991 was always going to make it.

I'd looked forward to the game for months – it's not every day that a full England team plays ten minutes from your house – and on the appointed day I'd arrived early, very early, to make sure of a good seat.

The moment I opened the programme, I immediately knew something was wrong. I wasn't feeling the usual excitement and found myself flicking through it without enthusiasm, barely registering the terrible illustrations on the cover and in the Pony Team Apparel advert. Even the realization that Graham Taylor, the England manager, had also managed Watford, the last team I'd seen play against New Zealand, almost a decade earlier, didn't get me reaching for my pen and notebook.

After just ten minutes, when Stuart Pearce hit a left-foot screamer from the edge of the box past a static Grant Schofield, I realized that I didn't even want to be there. The crowd seemed overwhelming, the noise frightening, and I found myself fighting for breath with a pounding headache. I just wanted to get out of the ground and get home. And so, less than halfway through the first half, I walked out of one of the most eagerly awaited games of my life.

As soon as I got home I took one of Caroline's nursing text-books from the shelf and diagnosed myself as having a tumour.

As I'd been feeling worse and worse, I thought I'd better go to the doctor and get a second opinion. He put it down to stress, but arranged a series of tests 'just to make sure'.

As it turned out, that was just the beginning. Over the next nine years my health went from bad to worse. My weight dropped alarmingly, breathing was a constant struggle, and I slept for all but six or seven hours a day. The doctors had no idea and the battery of tests turned up nothing. In desperation, I turned to less conventional treatments, from ear candling to bathing in Epsom salts. These steps were not a success.

In the end, my marriage collapsed and Caroline walked out. No one blamed her. I was impossible to live with. I also lost, in quick succession, my job, car and house. I moved to a pokey little flat around the corner, too ill to work. At one stage I even sold all my CDs just to get food. But however desperate things got, the one thing I could never bring myself to sell was my programme collection.

Friends stopped calling, and the only ones who kept in touch were those I'd known for quite a while. Kevin came over for a weekend, a round trip of twenty-four thousand miles. Birrell often rang for a chat, as did Dave, my oldest friend, who was now living in the US. He was going through a tough divorce and was just about broke, but that didn't stop him sending me $1,000 (and apologizing that it couldn't be more) when he found out I was being threatened with eviction.

Seeing the children every day was what kept me going, even though I missed all the milestones I'd been looking forward to so much, the things that I fondly remembered experiencing with my dad: the first day at school, going away on holiday together, and that all-important first football match. Instead, I proudly watched them grow from my bed.

But then, in 2000, I finally found out what was wrong with me. It was an unusual form of anaemia, and with the right treatment, I slowly began to recover. This was helped enormously by meeting Liz, an American woman who had fallen in love with New Zealand and who was able to see beyond my illness. We were married within a year of meeting and later rented a slightly bigger house, earning just enough to eat and pay the bills. I knew she was the one for me when she not only declined my offer to sell my programme collection so we could have a bit more money, but also kept me believing that I'd eventually recover.

And now, eight years after meeting her, I felt as though I might be well enough to make a journey. Liz's parents lived in Connecticut and they'd offered to put us up until we got back on our feet.

Naturally, I wanted to take my entire programme collection with me. It was only when it became clear that there would be no last-minute reprieve from Liz that I got down to the job of deciding which ones would accompany me to the US. The rest would be staying in New Zealand with Caroline, who had also remarried. Although we'd been divorced since the late nineties, we'd stayed friends and she'd volunteered to store them in her garage until we could afford to get them shipped over.

But for now, I had to concentrate on the ones I'd be taking. Once I'd carried out my initial cull, I was still left with over 150 serious candidates and I was seeing my pared-down collection in the same way that John West saw their fish, according to their TV commercial: it was the ones I was rejecting that would make the ones I was taking the best.

Reasoning that life isn't just about happy memories, I put that New Zealand v. England programme into the container Liz had allocated. I'd seen the early goal by Stuart Pearce that gave England the lead, but had missed Sheffield Wednesday's David Hirst adding a second for a comfortable 2–0 win. For many years I'd suspected this would be the last football match I'd ever see. I still thought it might be.

This programme was followed by more of the 'must haves', like Fulham against Manchester United – the first game I'd been to with my dad, who I hadn't seen in over twenty years. It was one of my greatest regrets that I hadn't gone back again when I still had my health, but the birth of the boys had pushed any thoughts of a long trip into the background. Now it looked as though I'd left it too late. Mum had written to me a few months earlier, saying that Dad had finally accepted that he'd never see me again.

As I carefully placed the programme in the container, I knew that if I managed to get to the US, I would also be able to make it home. An added incentive, as if I needed one, was that my daughter Hazel was now living in England and had recently had her first child, a son.

After that, the selection process started to get harder and some major highlights of the collection began to fall by the wayside as I was forced to get more and more brutal. The one programme I wavered over more than any other was Norway v. England from 1981, bought from David Stacey Publications via mail order. It was the most stat-heavy one I owned and I'd spent many a thoughtful hour analysing it. Although written in Norwegian, the parts that interested me were easy to under-stand as they were in the international language of statistics.

In the end, it came down to a simple choice: should I take England v. Norway (or Norge–England as it said on the cover), a technical triumph of a programme, or Crystal Palace v. Manchester United, a programme that reminded me that not all of my teenage crushes had turned out badly, only most of them? Typically, my heart ruled my head and Crystal Palace v. Manchester United won.

Another one that came perilously close to inclusion was the

Spurs v. Manchester United pirate programme. This had broken my young heart when I eagerly showed it off in the playground only to be told that it wasn't the real thing. But it had to be discarded in favour of the England Schools v. Germany Schools programme from the same era, which prompted fond memories of what had taken place on the field – a thrilling 2–1 England win – as well as the time I graduated from unlikely-to-lead-to-anything crushes (Betty Rubble from *The Flintstones*) to actual-living-person crushes (Susan from school).

George Best was also causing me serious angst, as he'd done to so many gaffers throughout his career. Eventually, Southampton v. Fulham won out over the Dunstable v. Luton 'souvenir programme' from 1975, which marked one of a handful of his appearances for the Southern League side. I'd hitchhiked to the first game and cycled to the second. Both reminded me of my devotion to the great man, but Southampton was the more memorable as I'd travelled for over seven hours to watch him sulkily slope off the pitch.

The last few suddenly became clear. As I flicked through the pages of the West Ham v. Hereford programme, I wondered what turn my life would have taken if I'd managed to stay on the tube and gone back to work that day instead of going to the game and losing my job. Bromley against the Civil Service was perfect confirmation that everyone, even Bromley, has their day, however long they have to wait for it, while Leeds v. Craiova and a couple of Plymouth programmes were a pleasant reminder that Caroline and I had had many good years before we divorced.

After putting the lid on the container, and making sure no programmes had been harmed in the process, I placed it carefully into the suitcase. I'd finished just in time – there was only an hour left before we had to leave. My sons Frank and Billy had helped us pack and would also be seeing us off. Even though they'd both left home, it had been important to me to get their blessing and they both seemed genuinely happy for me.

I began to relax, although not too much. I knew it was only a matter of time before I started reconsidering my selections. That was why I needed to distract myself before we left for the airport.

Then it came to me. I had just enough time to do something I'd half thought about doing for years – open the one tea chest that had sat in the garage unopened since it had been shipped over from England in 1982. It had DAVE MISCELLANEOUS scrawled on the side, and I couldn't resist having a peek inside.

In the midst of a bunch of old TV scripts, video cassettes (I hoped my disastrous WASS commercial wasn't among them) and T-shirts that would be far too small for me now I found the Christmas card from Plymouth Argyle. There was also a green and white scarf that Caroline had knitted me, plus some photos of my sister's dog Silas and my cats Pigdog and Sid.

And then, right at the bottom, looking old and chewed by Silas, was something that really brought home the passing of time. A small semi-circle of black plastic, a few inches wide, that had been untouched and neglected for decades. I tentatively took it out and stared at it as memories of a sunny spring day at Wembley came flooding back, of me desperately trying to impress Susan, who had displaced a Stone Age cartoon character in my affections. Was it really over forty years since I'd last taken the bat-a-rang from my utility belt?

But I resisted the temptation to wallow in nostalgia. Now was a time for looking forward, not back.

I was shaking with nerves as we drove to the airport, thirty-one of my most important programmes safely tucked away in the luggage. I hadn't been on a plane in over twenty years and was convinced I wouldn't be able to get on board. But the thought that this was a step closer to seeing my parents again gave me the strength to climb the stairs and take my seat on the plane.

I shut my eyes and gripped Liz's arm as we took off. Once we were in the air I began to relax, and when we touched down in Auckland I found myself looking forward to the adventure ahead of us. Each subsequent flight was easier, and by the time we arrived in Liz's home town of Hartford I knew I was now well enough to start living again.

Three weeks later, we stepped on board the 747 that would take us from Boston to London.

It was time to go home.

bromley

Official Match Day Programme 2008/09

FA Cup 2nd Qualifying Round Sponsored by E.ON.

AFC Hornchurch

Saturday 27th September , Kick off 3pm

£2

32

Bromley v. AFC Hornchurch,
27 September 2008

The FA Cup is so important for confidence in the team, and it's
important to the supporters to have a good cup run.

From the official programme

As we touched down at Heathrow and crawled slowly towards
the terminal, I looked out of the window and saw a couple of
ground crew sitting on a baggage container, drinking from
plastic cups and reading the *Sun*.

It felt good to be home.

The flight had been a far cry from the white-knuckle days.
As my health had improved, the fear of flying had disappeared,
and in its place was a feeling of excitement. This meant that I
hadn't slept on the flight, my mind restless with anticipation.
I couldn't wait to show Liz where I grew up, so she could see all
the places and meet the people I was always talking about.

But the first thing I did after clearing customs, as Liz
desperately searched for the nearest Starbucks, was find a pay-
phone and ring my parents. My dad sounded a bit surprised to
hear my voice, as though he hadn't allowed himself to believe I

was really coming home after so long. He wanted us to come over for tea the following day. He knew we'd be going to watch Bromley and preferred that we came round after that, so that they had time to prepare.

We picked up the car and drove through a series of half-familiar places, most changed almost beyond recognition. The hospital where I'd had my appendix out had been torn down, the pub I'd had my first drink in was now a restaurant, and the sweet shop near my primary school now sold mirrors. I felt disorientated, as though I was a stranger in my own hometown. Nothing seemed the same. The streets were more crowded, the roads more congested, and a huge shopping centre had sprung up in the middle of town.

The initial feeling of euphoria I'd had when touching down at Heathrow faded. Everything was different, and I felt as though I no longer belonged.

Finding the B&B was embarrassingly hard. Embarrassing because I'd told Liz that I knew exactly where it was; she didn't really believe my claim that 'it must have moved'. At least I had no problems finding the way to Bromley's Hayes Lane ground the following afternoon, even though this was the first time I'd driven anything other than a scooter there.

We parked outside, and as we walked up the long path towards the entrance, I suddenly stopped and stared.

'Are you OK?' Liz asked with a concerned look, seeing me struggling to keep it together.

How can you explain that surge of emotion that you get with that first glimpse of the floodlights as you walk towards a football ground? Especially if it's a ground with so many memories, and one you thought you'd never see again. I assured her that everything was fine, which probably would have been more convincing had a tear not been rolling down my face at the time.

The emotion was magnified when I bought my first official

matchday programmes in nearly twenty years. I was so over-
come with joy that I didn't realize they had cost me two quid
each. This made the one I had earmarked to add to my
collection easily the most expensive of the lot.

After paying a further £20 to get us in (that would have
bought something like fifteen season tickets last time I was
there), we were confronted by a man in his late fifties shouting
'Get your Golden Goal tickets here!' at anyone who was in the
vicinity. I recognized him as soon as I saw him, having stood
alongside him during countless Bromley defeats and the odd
win back in the seventies.

'Hello Roy,' I said. 'Remember me?'

'All right Dave?' he replied, as though he'd last seen me the
day before as opposed to thirty-two years ago.

I bought the last Golden Goal ticket from him and we sat
down together and talked about the old days. Liz was fascinated
to hear what kind of teenager I'd been and asked Roy plenty of
questions that he was only too happy to answer.

'I remember he always used to get two programmes,' Roy
told her, luckily failing to see that I was holding two programmes. 'We never could work out why.'

While they talked, I looked around, taking in sights that felt
reassuringly familiar. Although there had been a few cosmetic
changes over the years, it was still unmistakably Hayes Lane.
The benches behind the goal that The Grubby and I had sat on
for much of the late sixties and early seventies were still there,
and the terraces opposite hadn't changed beyond getting a fresh
lick of paint.

For the first time since setting foot on English soil again, I
felt at home.

As the teams ran out, it was bizarre to see players in the flesh
that I'd only seen fleetingly on YouTube, but it wasn't long
before the feelings of excitement and anticipation came

flooding back. The opposition, the grandly named AFC Hornchurch, played in the next division down and had only won one out of their last six matches. The last FA Cup game I'd seen at Hayes Lane was the 10–0 win against the Civil Service on a September day back in 1971. Even though this was so long ago that Alex Ferguson was then a striker for Falkirk, I was hoping for a similar result today.

The early signs gave every indication that I wouldn't be disappointed, as Bromley mounted a wave of attacks. The skill levels were much higher than anything I'd ever seen from a Bromley team. They could have been three up inside the first quarter of an hour, but it stayed goalless.

In the twentieth minute, a cross from Mark Janney, the Hornchurch winger, struck Adam Everitt ('a tenacious left-back' according to his profile) on the upper arm from point-blank range. The referee, Mr Nigel Lugg (Chipstead), pointed sternly to the spot. It was one of those penalties that some referees would give and others wouldn't.

'That's the kind of penalty some referees would give and others wouldn't,' explained the man sitting next to me to his shellshocked son, who was clutching his Bromley FC souvenir pen, the way I used to all those years ago.

My heart went out to the boy. I knew exactly the mix of confusion and pain he was going through as the Hornchurch striker tucked the ball neatly inside the right-hand post to give the visitors a 1–0 lead.

It was all too much for a middle-aged fan sitting behind us. 'How can that have been a penalty?' he screamed in Mr Lugg's direction. 'The law clearly states that it has to be deliberate!'

Murmurs of agreement greeted this outburst. I found myself nodding along, too. That's the thing about Bromley crowds. They've always gone for a more articulate and reasoned harassment of officials.

I wasn't too worried about the goal, though, as I remembered that the Civil Service had also dominated the early stages the last time I was there for a cup game, and then Bromley had put ten past them. But as the rest of the half took on a depressingly familiar pattern, Bromley attacking and Hornchurch defending with apparent ease, a feeling of foreboding came over me. This came with the realization that Bromley didn't actually have anyone who looked capable of scoring.

At half time, Liz and I sat with a couple of fellow old-timers who assured me that although the team were currently going through a rough time, a return to form was just around the corner. I remembered giving myself similar assurances all those years ago, on a weekly basis. The current problem was that they had got rid of their star striker for reasons no one could quite fathom and hadn't replaced him. It all had a familiar ring to it.

Although my original plan had been to save the programme until later, I couldn't resist a quick read through. It was a far more polished publication than I'd ever seen before at Hayes Lane and I felt proud that Bromley could now compete with the bigger clubs in such an important area.

The second half of this vital match carried on where the first half had left off. Bromley got a free kick just inside their own half, but it was not enough to appease the man behind us.

'Too late to try and make up for that penalty decision, ref!' he screamed. 'You're a disgrace!' He paused to allow the words to sink in before adding, 'A real disgrace!'

Liz nodded along in agreement.

By now I was beginning to sense that my optimism had been slightly misguided. One of the more common commentator's clichés is that the side that wins is the side that wants it most. And Hornchurch really did seem to want it a lot more – you could see the effort in the way they made every tackle and chased every lost cause. It was enough to make me reassess my expectations. I no longer needed a double-digit scoreline, I'd settle for a scrappy draw and a replay. I think most of the home crowd felt the same way.

Then, in the eightieth minute, came an incident that stopped the early leavers in their tracks and forced them back to their seats. The Hornchurch goalkeeper, Dale Brightly, who somehow merited two profiles in the programme, lost his bearings and handled outside the area. Mr Lugg, perhaps fearful of a certain crowd member, quickly produced a red card. The visitors' centre-half, Elliot Styles, took over in goal.

Ordinarily, this would have changed the direction of the match. To reiterate: home game, lower-league out-of-form opposition with ten men and no substitute goalkeeper.

My heart was still holding out hope, but my head knew different. I knew that there would be no late equalizer, no redemption. I felt for the fans around me, their faces lit up with expectation; I had mentally prepared myself for the array of near misses, great saves and inept finishing that followed. Finally, after an overgenerous amount of injury time, Mr Lugg blew his whistle and Bromley were out of the FA Cup for 2008/09.

I felt crushed. It was then that it struck me: I was still in love with Bromley, despite an absence of half a lifetime. In the way that a parent still loves a child who constantly lets them down, I found myself making excuses – that the game didn't really matter and the league was far more important, and if the referee hadn't given a penalty, which in my mind had gone from being a fifty–fifty call to an act of gross injustice, then we surely would have seen a home win.

In front of me a small gaggle of WAGs stood outside the tunnel, giggling. It was another shock. Glamorous women at Hayes Lane? Were Bromley players now considered a catch? My confusion only deepened when I saw them greet their AFC Hornchurch boyfriends.

As they wandered off to the bar, I took a last look around the club shop, which offered far more than it did the last time I'd been there. I bought a mug, a T-shirt and a woolly hat. Touchingly, Roy bought me an enamel badge. I even considered buying a DVD of the 2006 Kent Senior Cup Final 'with bonus footage of celebrations and presentation'. It was the only DVD on sale.

I couldn't have picked a better game to remind myself of what it was like being a Bromley fan. It had brought back feelings I'd banished to the far reaches of my memory. I knew I'd be back, and I knew it would be soon. But for now, with two pristine copies of the programme and a bag full of souvenirs, it was time to leave Hayes Lane and complete the journey home.

As I looked back at the ground, which was bathed in autumn sunshine, I heard a lone voice coming from inside. 'Hurry up, ref,' it said in a tired yet belligerent tone, the words echoing around the empty terraces, 'your Hornchurch mates are in the bar, waiting to buy you a drink.'

We got into the car. Liz had to drive as I was so nervous about the reunion with my parents, which was now only minutes away. Would they be disappointed with the way my life had worked out? Would we be able to carry on where we left off? It was the best part of twenty-two years since I'd last seen them and I didn't know how much I'd changed in that time.

As we weaved our way through the backstreets of Bromley, I carefully placed the programmes between the covers of the AA roadmap and my thoughts drifted back to the day I'd held a programme for the first time, at the age of nine. I remembered standing proudly alongside my dad on the terraces at Fulham as I eagerly flicked through the pages, excited at seeing familiar names like Haynes and Marsh, Best and Charlton, thrilled at discovering that Johnny Haynes used the same vinyl football as I did, and savouring the smell of freshly printed paper.

My mind snapped back to the present as we pulled up out-side the house, a small maisonette in a quiet, leafy cul-de-sac. My heart started pounding even faster when I saw my dad standing at the window. I wondered how long he'd been there. He was smaller than I remembered, and hunched over, but still, despite being in his eighty-ninth year, immaculately dressed in jacket and tie. Although nearly blind, he was peering out, a look of hope on his face.

As I took a deep breath, Liz gently stroked my arm. 'Go on,' she said. 'It's what you've been waiting for.'

Not wanting to wait a moment longer, I jumped out of the car and started walking, then jogging, down the path to the front door.

Acknowledgements

Thanks to Giles Elliott for his enthusiasm and wisdom, my agent Kate Hordern for finding the perfect editor for this book, (Dave) Birrell for patiently reading everything I sent him and frequently nudging me in the right direction, Tom Bromley, who was so generous with his time and expertise in helping develop the idea, David Hayes for his advice and for being part of my story for over forty years, Caroline and Richard Harkett for kindly looking after the rest of my collection, Charlie Connelly for the encouragement, Derek Dobson, Nick Frost, Steve Garthwaite and John Self for remembering things I'd long forgotten, and to Gabriel and Nancy Noli for all they've done for us.

Dave Roberts has been one of those annoying bike couriers, a security guard, a civil servant, a KFC chef who was fired for trying to steal a sample of the secret recipe and a train driver – all before reaching the age of twenty. After that, he settled for a career in advertising, which was eventually cut short by illness, but not before accidentally winning a Silver Lion at Cannes. He now writes books, which all seem to have a theme in common: obsession . . .

If you'd like to get in touch with Dave, please email him at dave@daverobertsbooks.com or visit www.daverobertsbooks.com